# Matilda Gundalini

# Matilda Gundalini

*A Tale of Workplace Harassment*

SUSAN MORESI

# DEDICATION

To HB Buchanan who always said her name *should* be
Matilda Gundalini.

# CONTENTS

# CHAPTER 1

# *We Meet Mr. Braddock*

We were in a van driving back to the office having spent half-a-day at a conference that was still going on without us. The conference was in Vickerton, about 50 miles away from our office in Rockleburg. Our new boss, Herman Braddock was driving, having insisted that he be the driver, both ways. He had become our boss, I guess officially he's our supervisor, just a few weeks before, due to his promotion. For the two or three years just prior to this very recent promotion, he'd been the supervisor of a smaller office in Boise, Idaho. I was trying to give the guy a chance, but even after just two weeks I wasn't getting the feeling that I was going to enjoy working for him.

There is no easy, direct route between Vickerton, where the conference was, and our office in Rockleburg, so now we were driving back to Rockleburg on a two-lane road. We passed some kind of a second-hand shop with a bunch of not-nice-looking used furniture out in front. For God-only-knows-what reason, Ken, one of my co-workers, yelled to Herman from the back seat, "Hey Herman, here's where you can get some furniture for your new house. You could probably get a deal!"

I was kind of surprised that Ken would talk to any boss, and especially a new boss, like that. I don't really like these personal digs. I guess I expected Herman to just ignore the comment, but he yelled back, just as loudly, "I never pay full price for anything I buy." He then went on to explain that whenever he makes a major purchase, like furniture, "I always talk them down on the price or I get them to throw in something extra."

Herman's comment bothered me, and even though we'd only been working together for a couple of weeks I felt this newly-familiar feeling that something wasn't right. His *attitude* bothered me. I mean, here we were over a year into the 21ˢᵗ century and Herman was making something like $80,000.00 a year. I just couldn't stop thinking of some poor furniture salesman having to give up his measly commission, or part of it, so that Herman could feel like a big shot. There was a little more discussion in the van about the furniture and Herman buying it and then we came back around to the not paying full price idea and I said (I guess you could say without thinking) "Well Herman, *I* think that's *gauche.*" The van immediately became silent, and I somehow felt that Herman, more than not liking the comment, didn't know what that meant. Honestly, I wouldn't have known what it meant either if my sister hadn't taken French in high school, but I didn't feel like explaining. We kept driving and chatting, but nothing more was said about Herman buying furniture. Eventually, we got back to the office.

It was only about two o'clock when we arrived back at the office, so there was still plenty of workday left. I was sitting in my cubicle a couple of hours later when Karen walked over. "Matilda," she sort of whispered "I was just talking to Ken and Sarah about your little outing this morning. You didn't tell Herman he was *gauche,* did you?"

There was a little pause as I thought about this. "W-e-l-l-l-l, I guess I did," I dragged out my answer.

Karen's eyes widened quite a bit. "Matilda!" she gasped, her right hand going to her chest just below her neck "You can't do that!"

This seemed like a bit of an overreaction to me. "Is it that big a deal, Karen?" I asked.

"Well, I know for a fact he doesn't like that kind of thing," she responded, her voice sounding decidedly calmer. "*I* wouldn't talk to him like that; he won't forget it, I can tell you that."

Karen was one of the people who had known Herman before he had come to work in Rockleburg.  About 8 or 10 years ago, Herman had some kind of a not-too-high-level job at a regional headquarters somewhere on the west coast, and at that time, Karen had worked in some field office out there.

"Did they tell you how this started?" I asked her.  "We drove past some dumpy, second-hand store and Ken yelled to the whole van that Herman should buy the used, beat-up furniture there because it would probably be cheap.  The next thing I know, Herman is bragging about how he never pays full price for anything.  It was kind of sick."

"I just wanted to warn you, Matilda, that Herman wants us to act like he's the boss, *all the time,* and especially in public!" she continued.  She turned to walk out of my cubicle, and as she was leaving, she said: "But you do what you want, Matilda, it's your funeral."

And then I got flowers.  I hadn't been thinking about it being Valentine's Day at all.  I had been so preoccupied with getting to this conference this morning and the people I wanted to see there and whatever, but I got flowers.  My boyfriend Roy had sent me a little, desk-sized tea rose bush in a pot.  It was a nice little plant, and it was nice to have flowers sent to me at work.  I'm not sure I'd ever gotten flowers at work before.

I met Roy at a local trivia group, and we ended up on the same team.  I guess it was over a year ago  now.  We did kind of hit it off.  When I met Roy, he was still going through his divorce.  He has two daughters who are now 16 and 11.  The whole time I've known Roy, we really have kept me pretty much separate from them.  I mean, they know about me, and I've met them, but when I met him things weren't going well between him and his about-to-be ex, and neither Roy nor I thought the girls needed any more to worry about.  I still kind of feel that way.  I mean, they have two parents who love them, and they see them and can talk to either of them at any time.  Things are still not great between Roy and his ex-wife, Laura, and I just think him having a girlfriend (me) doesn't give either of the girls a happy feeling.  So, actually, no problem.  I mean, I do see them, although not that often, and I hear about them, and Roy sees them and talks to them quite a bit, but I don't really feel like we all need to be together all the time. I wouldn't mind seeing them more, but I do think it's a lot for them—they start feeling disloyal to their mother, they report things to her, and it's just not that great. According to Roy, before there was any talk about divorce things weren't really wonderful between him and Laura. They were both trying to make things better, until one night at supper the younger girl, Tina, said "Mommy, since Daddy has to work on Friday is Mr. Ted going to come over to watch a movie again and are we going to have popcorn like last time?" I don't think things ever got better after that.

Anyhow, back at work, two or three people commented about my little rose bush in the little flowerpot, and at the very end of the day Herman was walking by my cubicle, saw the flowers, and stopped to talk about them. He said something about it being nice to get flowers and I think he added in something about "Who's the lucky fellow?" at the end. It was a perfectly nice conversation, but it did occur to me later as I walked out to my car, that that little conversation and the discussion about the beat-up furniture and the "I think it's *gauche*" comment were the only conversations I'd had with Herman all day.

I work for a government contractor called Health Solutions and Office Oversight (HSOO), Inc. We pronounced it "HIS-zoo." We do a lot of work for private healthcare organizations, but we also do ALOT of contract work for the Department of Health and Human Services. We keep in touch with healthcare providers, but not all healthcare providers. Some of our clients call with questions about getting government services for their patients, and we advise them. Some of our clients have become our clients because patients or insurance companies have complained about them. Some of our clients *are* insurance companies whose records we reviewed. You get the picture. Anyhow, HSOO has several offices around the country, but these offices really vary in size.

A few months after Herman's arrival, the whole "I think that's *gauche*" comment, and the getting flowers at work thing, I started realizing, for some reason, that I was now about halfway through my sixth year of working for HSOO, and halfway through my fifth year as a healthcare facilitator. I had started with HSOO as an administrative aide to a Mr. Dormier in procurement, and about eight months later he voluntarily transferred to a job in Florida. Once Mr. Dormier had moved to the office in Florida and they were looking for someone to replace him, I started hearing rumblings that the acting head of procurement wasn't sure if he wanted to retain the administrative aide position (me). Luckily, the job I'm in now had opened up in the healthcare facilitation department right around that time, and I got that job, which is this job, and which at that time had been a promotion for me. Not all that long after I started in this job, HSOO did re-organize the procurement department, and they did eliminate that administrative aide position, so I'm glad I had found another job, or maybe they helped me find this position, I've never been entirely sure. I'm saying all of this to get to the point that I've been in my current job for over five years. From working in the two departments here at HSOO and from other work experience I've had, and, in fact from the jobs I've had where I supervised people, I know that different supervisors have different styles, emphasize different things, etc., but some things are usually somewhat consistent from job to job. For example, in both departments that I've worked in here at HSOO and at most of the other places where I've worked, we've always had meetings from time to time to discuss news, policy changes, give status reports, etc. However, I am now finding the Herman Braddock style to be, let's say, kind of different than what I have been used to. For example, one of the first meetings he called has come to be known as the "I went to see a play" meeting. Here's the way I remember it:

About a month or two after Herman had started in our office, and we were all adjusting to him as our new boss, he called a meeting. I don't remember what the meeting was about, but my co-workers and I certainly do remember the ending. The meeting was winding up, and for some reason, Herman started talking about how he had gone to see a play within the last week or so. He mentioned the play and that he was trying to get to know the city of Rockleburg, to get out and socialize, and that he thought he was kind of settling in. Then, out of the clear blue, Herman said something like, "You guys are going to have to help me find some eligible women to socialize with," and then he winked! If nothing else, I think he got our attention.

I'll just describe my reaction as very surprised. I thought that I'd had quite a few bosses over my career, some nice ones, a few jerks, and plenty not really memorable, but I don't remember any boss, or ever hearing of any boss who sat in front of all of his subordinates and asked them for help finding a date. But do you know what? Once he said that I actually couldn't help thinking about possible girlfriends for Herman. I mean, I thought he might really be lonely. And maybe that was his way, awkward, but his way, of trying to ask for help.

A week or so later, I ran into Nelia, a woman who worked in an office down the hall, and it occurred to me that she might be a good match for Herman. She was nice enough, our work was similar, and she seemed kind of religious. I started thinking that they might be a good couple. Just as an aside, my matchmaking in the past has been, I think without exception, disastrous. I ran into Karen around this time and told her my excellent matchmaking idea. "He won't want to go out with her," Karen pronounced.

"Why not?" I asked, and delineated my list of her positive attributes.

"Because she's not, you know, perfect enough. Herman wants someone, maybe not obedient, but very agreeable, and preferably really good-looking," Karen told me.

"Well, I hate to tell him Karen, but he's not exactly every woman's dream," I said, defending my great idea, although I guess I already knew it was a failure. "And she *is* good looking," I continued, still defending Nelia and my idea.

"She's not bad looking or hard to get along with Matilda, but it's not that," Karen went on. "He wants like a showstopper, you know, perfect in every way."

"Well, I don't think of Herman as Prince Charming, Karen," I kept explaining, for no really good reason. "And he's not exactly Mr. Easygoing either," I added.

"He's been divorced three times," Karen told me.

"Three times!" I kind of yelled.

"Well, maybe it's only twice, I'm not sure. But he does have two or three children; I mean, I'm sure they're at least in there 20's by now." There was a pause, then Karen looked at me, shrugged her shoulders, and said: "You've met the guy, Matilda, I mean he's..., he's..., you know..., odd."

I just couldn't let this go. "Well, why did he ask us to help him find a date, Karen? I mean, that's weird." I just had to ask her.

"I guess he wants companionship," she said, kind of smiling and went walking toward the coffeepot.

As far as I know, Herman and Nelia never went on a date or had virtually any social interaction. Humph!

So life with Herman as our boss continued for the next several months. During this time, it seemed like there was never a shortage of examples of Herman appearing to have no idea what he was doing. It really wasn't a situation I liked. Angela, the supervisor that Herman replaced, had been so nice and easy to work with, and frankly, even after I guess it's going on 8 or 9 months now, I was *still* finding working for Herman to be quite an adjustment. Herman routinely made terrible policy decisions, said a lot of things that either didn't make sense or were hard to understand, and based on what went on at our staff meetings, he seemed to enjoy making fun of people, especially in front of other people. On the bright side, there had never been any *official* change to our jobs as healthcare facilitators or of the jobs of any of the other healthcare facilitators across the country, so we all continued doing what we had been doing, with the added frequent annoying interference and ridiculous ideas for "improvements" from Herman.

I'll give you an example: One nice, nice, fall day I was sitting in my cubicle when my phone rang. The caller ID showed Herman Braddock. I picked up the phone and he said: "Matilda, I'd like to talk to you about your travel arrangements for this meeting in Chicago next month."

"Ok," I said.

"We'll be traveling together," he said.

"Ok," I said.

"Benita can give you the specifics of my flight and hotel arrangements, and I'd like you to coordinate yours with mine. We might as well go together," he said.

Now, people in our division travel quite a bit, and it's not at all unusual for any of us to go together (or alone, for that matter). Usually, when traveling with Mr. Braddock (or even Angela in the good ol' days), Benita, our supervisor's secretary, would make our supervisor's travel arrangements, and then we'd request the same flight, hotel, or whatever we needed. It was entirely normal for any of us to get these arrangements from Benita, and then to make matching arrangements, as it were. If a rental car was involved, usually Benita would arrange it, and we'd all use the same car when we got there. Of course, since Herman's arrival, Herman would almost always drive and would almost always insist he knew where he was going, and he almost always did not, so frequently, the trip would start with getting lost, frustration, name-calling, hard feelings, and something close to exhaustion.

"Ok," I said, "Is anyone else going to this meeting?"

"Yes," he said, "there will be two other individuals attending the meeting with us, but we'll be traveling Wednesday night, and they'll be arriving later in the week."

Among his many other annoying habits, Herman's use of the English language drove me nuts. Why would my boss call my co-workers "other individuals?" It's not like we don't know each other; we've all been working together for years. What does he mean "other individuals?" Is there some reason he doesn't want me to know who's going? I really can't tell if he goes out of his way to make things confusing, or this is just how he talks. It's very annoying. "Ok, Herman," I said, "I'll get the scoop from Benita and make my arrangements."

"Matilda, I would appreciate it if you would make your arrangements in the next day or two so I can approve them, and we can finalize this travel," Herman told me. "Monica, who's coordinating this meeting in Chicago, needs a definite headcount and needs information about when people are arriving, and I'd like to be able to give that to her as soon as possible," he continued.

"Ok, Herman. I'll get it done today. So are you thinking we'll take a car from here and go to the airport together?" I asked.

"Well, I don't know about all that, Matilda," Herman replied.

Now, what on earth does *that* mean? Once again, I had no understanding, and to be honest, I kind of prided myself on understanding people, or at least I used to before I met Mr. Braddock. If we're not going to drive to the airport together, why are we knocking ourselves out to get on the same flight? There aren't even that many flights from our area in Kansas to Chicago anyway; we'd almost inevitably end up on the same flight. Why would we take two separate cars the 35 miles to the airport (and back), not that I wouldn't prefer driving my own car, but it seemed, let's say, not the normal way we'd do this. I swear I cannot understand this guy at least 50% of the time, and I don't think it's me. I just keep thinking, "Herman, Communication Is Key!"

So, get this! Later in the afternoon I walked to Benita's desk and asked about Herman's travel plans. She looked confused and said, "There are no plans yet, Matilda. He told me to hold off making his plans because he's not sure what days he wants to travel."

Is this what work is supposed to be like? You spend all day trying to figure out what your boss is trying to say? After a moment, I told her he had called me about 4 hours ago and told me to make sure to get on the same flight that he was taking, and pretty much to make it snappy. We looked at each other. Finally, I said, "Well, I guess when he decides, could you let me know?"

Benita shrugged and said, "I guess."

As I say, these kinds of conversations drive me nuts. I really don't remember conversations like this before Mr. Braddock showed up, or really at any other time in my life. By the way, it took Herman so long to make his travel arrangements that I couldn't get a room at the same hotel. Somehow the other two "individuals" from our office got rooms in the same hotel as Herman, and it turned out, most of the other meeting attendees did, too. The one I stayed at was only a couple blocks away, and I liked it better because it had a little kitchenette.  Once Herman found out about my staying at a different hotel and my kitchenette, he just wouldn't stop bringing it up.  For some reason, he made several comments during this trip to me and about me in front of many others about the kitchenette, how I needed a kitchenette, couldn't live without a kitchenette, why did I need a kitchenette, and how did I like my kitchenette.  (Honestly, I liked it.)

# CHAPTER 2

# *Trip to Chicago*

So, after quite a bit of back and forth, Herman and I did end up going together, in a HSOO car, from the office to the airport. Why this would require about 5 separate conversations to plan, I still don't know, but it did. Of course Herman drove, which was ok with me, but he did make a big deal about how he was going to drive, he doesn't feel safe if he's not driving, blah, blah, blah. Ok Herman, you can drive the car. What is the big deal?

It was November when we went to Chicago. The meeting was held to generate input from "the field" for our bosses at HSOO headquarters in Pennsylvania on some pretty significant policy issues. According to Monica, the coordinator, it had been a nightmare to schedule, so even when we did meet, it was over a weekend, from a Wednesday through a Monday. There were people at this meeting from several offices, including people from Chicago (of course), 4 of us from our office in Rockleburg, and, among the many others, Tanya, who was there from the Boise office.

HSOO has 10 offices around the country that all do the same type of work we do, so it's our office plus 9 other offices. As I've said, all of these offices perform the same function, but because over the past 10 or 15 years HSOO has closed offices, consolidated offices, opened satellite offices, etc., the offices are actually radically different in size. The largest office, in Pensacola, Florida has something like 40 or 45 healthcare facilitators, and a couple of the smaller ones, one somewhere in New England and one, I can't remember where, somewhere in the southwest I think, are made up of something like 8 or 10 healthcare facilitators. Herman had been Tanya's supervisor in the 12-person (I think) Boise, Idaho office for a couple of years just before he got promoted to the job in our office in Rockleburg, Kansas which is a bigger office (there are positions for 22 healthcare facilitators in Rockelburg, but not all of the positions are filled all of the time). Several months ago, not that long after Herman had become our boss, there was some reason I had to call Tanya, and we kind of hit it off. She was actually pretty knowledgeable about contacting healthcare providers and had great suggestions about specific, tactful language to use, and she also complained about Herman quite a bit, which I enjoyed. Anyway, as far as actual work getting done at this meeting in Chicago, the Pennsylvania headquarters people wanted so many decisions from us that we decided the best thing to do was to keep breaking up into smaller groups and then to present our small-group conclusions to the whole group. There was a lot of discussing and arguing and convincing going on during this 5 - day meeting.

On Sunday, I ran into Tanya in the cafeteria, and she told me that she'd been in a small group with Herman the day before and that it had been just terrible. I couldn't wait to hear more. Apparently, their small group had met in a conference room with a TV set, and Herman had insisted on having some football game on with the volume blaring. "I forgot what it was like to work with him," she said. "No one could concentrate the whole time we were in there," she went on. "He said that if he had to work on a Saturday, at least he was going to listen to the game," Tanya continued. "It was unbelievable," she said. "I mean, come on Matilda, we had to *volunteer* to come to this meeting. If he didn't want to come, why did he come? My God, Matilda, it was just miserable being in that room with him."

It must've been that night because, as I recall, I had already heard the football game story from Tanya, so I guess that made it Sunday night (or maybe, technically, early Monday morning). A bunch of us had gone to dinner together, including Tanya and Herman, who got into a loud argument in the restaurant about whether or not it was hard to be a cashier at a fruit stand, which Tanya had done during the summers when she was in college. The dinner, not counting the Tanya and Herman loud, attention-getting discussion, was pretty nice. If nothing else, the food was good. When I left to go to my hotel, it seems like someone was trying to get some people to go out for a drink or two since this was our last night in Chicago, but I wasn't interested, and I don't really remember who was talking or what they decided. I left; that's what I knew.

I was asleep in my hotel room somewhere around midnight or one a.m. (I'm really not sure about the time) when the phone in my room rang. I answered it, and a woman said: "This is Patricia from the front desk." At least that's the way I remember it.

"Yes," I said, having no idea what this could be about.

"There's a man here who wants to come up to your room. Should I send him up?" she asked.

I don't know exactly what I said, but I think it was something on the order of "What?"

I think she just about repeated what she had said. "There's a man here who wants to come up to your room. But we don't give out room numbers without getting your permission. Would you like me to send him up?"

Now, this took a little thought. Of course, I didn't want some hotel in Chicago sending some guy up to my room at 1 a.m. (or really any other time), but who could this be, and what could this be about?

I said, "Who is it?"

She said in a somewhat annoyed tone, "It's a man who wants to come up to your room."

"I get that," I said, "but who is it?" I asked again.

Now, as I recall, she said, not to me, "Sir, she wants to know your name." and I swear I heard a voice that sounded just like Herman's saying, "Thanks man, thanks for that."

Then a different man's voice said: "Oh, no problem."

Then there was a pause, and the woman said to me, "Well, he's gone." There was a little pause, and then we both hung up.

I don't know whether I should've found this more unsettling than I did, but I was tired, and we had to check out the next morning, and I was going to have to take my luggage to the office and I just, I guess you'd say, had other stuff on my mind (like primarily, sleeping.) She had said he was gone, whatever that was about. Right about this time, I heard the ding of the elevator down the hall outside my room, and then footsteps, kind of heavy footsteps, or at least I thought I did. Not loud. Then there was a tap on my door. I could see the shadow of shoes or something in the little light coming under the door from the hallway. Could this be Herman? I couldn't believe it. Surely this guy wouldn't show up at my hotel room late at night, would he? I mean, we are not friendly. We haven't agreed on virtually anything since I met him. This can't be. I never left the bed, and after maybe 14 seconds, the shoes went away. It was just that one tap on the door. I'm sure of that, plus I remember the shoes, or what seemed like shoes. What just happened? Apparently, I went back to sleep.

The next morning, when I was checking out (I had to wait for a cab anyhow), I asked the desk clerk, whose name tag said "Patricia" if she had worked overnight. She said, "Yes, we've been here all night."

I said, "Well, who was that guy that wanted to come to my room?" She knew nothing or certainly didn't want to get involved.

She said, "What guy?"

I said, "Someone called me, a woman, from the front desk somewhere around midnight and said there was a man who wanted to come to my room. What was that about?" I asked.

Patricia repeated (I swear they learn this in front desk training) "What guy?" I repeated my question. She said, "Oh, you mean that really drunk guy?"

I said, "What?"

She said, "There was a guy here around one o'clock who was really drunk. You know, anyone can walk into this lobby, and sometimes people get confused; they're in the wrong hotel or something."

I said, "I don't know if he was really drunk. A woman called my room and asked about giving out my room number."

She said, "The guy was really drunk. And we would never send someone like that to someone's room without getting permission."

I said, "I heard his voice, and it sounded like he was talking to someone else here, like a man.  I heard the person say "Thanks, man" and a man's voice responded."

She said, "I think that's your cab."  I looked at her for several seconds, and then, basically, I left.

I did tell Roy about this incident.  If nothing else, I had been doing my share (at least) of complaining to him about Herman. Roy seemed to think about this for a while, many seconds, a lot longer than he thought about most things before responding. Then he said, "It was probably him."

I said loudly, "What!"

He said, "It was probably him."

"Oh Roy, don't say that," I responded.  "Just say 'Oh Matilda, that's ridiculous;  no one is going to come to your room late at night....'"

"Suit yourself, Matty," Roy said.  "But I don't think there are too many people in Chicago who knew you were staying at that hotel and apparently, someone asked for you, by name."

I said, "Why would he do that?  I mean, we really don't get along.  There are tons of people we both know at this meeting."

Roy repeated again, "It had to be someone you know."

I reviewed this in my mind.  Patricia was of absolutely no help and honestly seemed to be trying to save herself.  Someone came to my door, I'm sure.  Who and why I don't know.  The drunk part, I don't know what to make of that.

About a month after this whole thing, the Chicago trip and the weird and probably-should've-been-more-upsetting situation at night in the hotel, so, it must've been around December, I started noticing that Herman was assigning me lots and lots of little jobs, and some not - so - little jobs.  In some cases, the ones I noticed most, he seemed to be just trying to annoy me.  He would call and say, "Matilda, go down to the mailroom and see if they have any mail for me," even though our mail got delivered to us by the mailroom workers.

Co-workers of mine, including Karen, had started coming to me and asking what I had done to Herman.  Two of the woman who approached me actually *worked in a different division*, although our cubicles were "co-located" with theirs. I told them I hadn't done anything. They'd make comments like "He sure seems to have it in for you," or "Well, something's bugging him," or, my favorite, "You must've done something!"

A few months after these little (or big) extra jobs started happening, so, it would've been toward the beginning of the next year, a few months after this Chicago trip, when we were trying to make hotel reservations for a different trip, I was reminded of this nighttime incident, and I told Karen about it. I included that I was sure I had heard a voice that sure did sound like Herman's, which is kind of distinctive. I don't know what I expected, but her reaction surprised me: She said: "Oh, you're just so attractive Matilda, no one can resist you."

I said, "No Karen, I'm not saying…" but she butt in.

"Herman is not interested in you, Matilda," she began. "I'm telling you, he has a type. And you ain't it. And your story really doesn't make much sense anyhow. Some guy comes into a hotel in Chicago, of all places and just begs for YOUR room number! And then, conveniently, the woman at the desk "forgets" that she called you." As Karen turned and left my cubicle, she made some kind of comment like "Ay, ay, ay" or something threw her hands up into the air. So much for sharing with officemates.

# CHAPTER 3

# *I Get Surprises*

The new year had started and working with Herman continued to be just weird, or hard to understand, or something. It wasn't just Herman and me either. Plenty of people, but now that I think about it, not everyone, had complaints about Herman, his nutty (to be polite) decisions, how he could come up with ideas to waste money, how he'd make plans for something and include everyone except one or two people: he'd give awards to virtually everyone in the office but leave out one or two people, to either hurt their feelings or just to make his feelings really obvious, etc. And we didn't really get used to it. I mean, we weren't surprised that there seemed to constantly *be* nutty ideas and nutty instructions from the boss, but still, I think it's fair to say that the individual nutty ideas themselves were typically pretty surprising. And then there were these meetings that seemed to start out as a normal meeting, get through the middle as a normal meeting, and then take a weird turn at the end.

In one meeting around that time, all of us in the Healthcare Provider Facilitation division were in the conference room. For most of the meeting, nothing was at all unusual. At the end of the meeting, as people were getting up and leaving, Herman, who was standing by the doorway and almost directly in front of the light switch called to me and said, "Matilda, would you make sure the lights get turned off?" I looked up from a handout I was re-reading. There had to be at least 8 people, *and Herman*, sitting or standing closer to the light switch than I was, but "Ok," I thought, "I guess I can."

Approximately 15 seconds later, Herman said: "Well Matilda, aren't you going to turn out the lights?"

I tried to figure out what the guy wanted, then said: "Herman, I was waiting for people to leave the room." Apparently, Herman found this to be argumentative.

"Did I tell you to wait for people to leave, Matilda?" Herman said, forcefully enough that several conversations stopped, and people started walking toward the door. "If he's trying to confuse me, he's succeeding," I thought.

"No Herman," I answered, "you didn't tell me to wait."

"It seems to me Matilda," he said, "that you like to make your own rules." I like to make my own rules? Ok, the meeting was over, there were several people in the conference room, and Herman was standing *right in front of the light switch.* No one had ever mentioned anything about lights at any other meeting we'd ever had. Why was he involving me? I'll say one thing, although all of this was happening in plain sight, it didn't seem to bother anyone. So I 1) got up, 2) excused myself as I passed several people, 3) walked toward Herman and the light switch, 4) passed Herman and 5) flipped the light switch, and 6) the lights went off. The whole thing (steps 1 – 6 above) did not seem to make him happy. I have no explanation of this entire incident, like 1) why it happened, 2) what was the purpose, 3) why he asked me to do that, because he *was* standing right in front of the light switch, 4) etc.

Furthermore, this is the kind of thing I mean about working with Herman being weird. I don't really have a better word. I can't believe how this guy wastes time all the time. I do have work to do. What's the big deal with lights all of a sudden? I started resigning myself to the idea that this is now my life at HSOO, which used to be such a nice place to work.

The spring was our division's busy time, so for the next several months we were swamped. It was hard to get time off, people were coming in early, working through lunch, staying late, even coming in on weekends. If you didn't do some of that, you were just crazy during the regular work week, so almost everyone put in some kind of extra time. I don't know if you'd say we were exhausted, but we were busy. This happened every spring. So, I'm going to say that no one expected Herman's announcement at a meeting he called during this time.

Herman had emailed us all to meet him in the conference room and had given us about 10 minutes notice. This by itself is not that unusual; sometimes he had some kind of news that he just wanted to make sure everyone understood and it only took a minute or two to communicate. It just wasn't that weird. But what was weird was that in the middle of all this stress (and, as I say, this was an every spring thing), Herman announced that he wanted us all to go to a ballgame on Friday night. He said we all needed some stress relief. As I think was becoming usual, first there was disbelief as we each thought, "A ballgame? Like now? In the middle of all of this?" Then there was denial. Like "He can't be suggesting a ballgame. Is he saying to leave work on Friday after a day of all this and go to a ballgame at night? With him? And somehow, we're going to relax?" Then there was a kind of, I guess you could call it acceptance, like "I guess he's telling us to go with him to a ballgame." Then people started trying, in their minds, to restructure their weekends: activities with children and grandchildren, church activities, shopping, etc. And then a few brave souls tried to make excuses such as "I can't go, I'm going to a family reunion," or "I wish I could Herman, but I just can't Friday night, our pastor is leaving, and we're having his farewell dinner on Friday." Some of these excuses were believable, and some were not, and after a while, I got the idea that maybe some of these people were trying to outdo Herman with their weird ideas. I think they enjoyed making up these stories, or perhaps they were true, although very coincidental. I have never been able to figure that out.

So, we went to a ballgame. There's actually a triple-A baseball team in Rockleburg and a nice stadium. Roy grudgingly went with me, and later I more or less agreed with him that it's not fun for anyone to spend their (limited) free time with their not-fun boss, but we went. For whatever reason, I can barely remember the game or even the evening. I remember Roy and me driving to the stadium and kind of sitting with the group. I don't remember much of the game, and while I think everyone who attended, which was most of our division, tried to be nice to each other, I'm not sure anyone wouldn't have rather been home — or doing something else, primarily without Herman. But, as far as I can remember, it was ok. I think it taught me for absolute certain not to go to any other social outings with Herman. Oh, and one other thing: I also recall that as we were all trying to politely say "Good-night" and get out of there, that Herman made some kind of comment like "I've never seen so many ingrates! After I pay to take you all to a ballgame. No one is even thanking me! Next time you can all pay for your own tickets!"

Back at work, we got through our busy season. Once that's over, lots of people typically take a week or two of vacation. This means that work is *still* busy because every week for several weeks, a number of people are on vacation, and everyone who's left is doing their own work, helping out the vacationers' work, and trying to plan their own vacations.

And that brings us to what I like to call the Alaskan Cruise Incident. In hindsight, there is no explanation for this. It's possible that an objective person could conclude that the whole thing was my fault, but let's move on from that. I don't know what I was thinking (well, I sort of do), or how this could've happened, but it did. The Alaskan cruise was fun, but this whole thing leading up to it, as I say, possibly all my fault, was just nutty. I can only explain it by saying that I think some of Herman's nuttiness was wearing off on me. Or maybe there was some weird astrological situation or sunspots or something else going on that was responsible. Whatever the cause, it really happened.

Everyone at work seemed to be planning vacations, talking about vacations, going on vacations, etc., and I got the idea that Roy and I should take a cruise to Alaska. They really weren't that expensive, and I decided this was a great idea (which it was). I don't know why, but for some reason I started thinking that it would be fun if a bunch of us from work went on a cruise together. My idea really didn't make much sense because, of course, a bunch of us (there were a total of 18 healthcare facilitators in the Rockleburg office at that time) couldn't all be gone at the same time. I don't know why I started this "we'll all go to Alaska" campaign at work, but I did. Maybe I was just tired or slap happy. Whatever it was, I started telling my cubicle neighbors that Roy and I were probably going to go on a cruise to Alaska, that it wasn't going to be that expensive, and that they should come. Absolutely "to a man," as they say, no one was interested. They said it cost too much, they'd either have to or wouldn't be able to take their kids (or parents), they had other plans, etc. Overall and without a doubt, virtually none of my co-workers was the least bit interested in going on a cruise to Alaska. At least not this summer, or at least not with me and Roy.

Except Herman. Somehow, I had forgotten all about him. On one of these days when I was still, half- jokingly (but not all the way jokingly) trying to recruit people to go on the cruise, Herman came walking by my cubicle, and I guess overheard me and who-knows-who talking about a possible cruise to Alaska. As with many things Herman, the conversation probably couldn't have gone worse.

Herman said: "Alaska, I've always wanted to go to Alaska."

I said something like, "Well, this might be a good time." The way I remember it, I was thinking that surely this wouldn't work out and he wouldn't be able to go. He's got to work, after all. And he's cheap. And he probably doesn't want to get on a ship, because *he wouldn't be able to drive.* I don't think I consciously thought of any of this. I was just trying not to offend him (once again) and I was just sure (or hoping) that this couldn't possibly happen. I mean, I had suggested it to at least 6 or 8 other people thinking it was a real possibility and none of them was even mildly interested. But, apparently, once again, when it came to Herman, I was dead wrong.

Herman didn't end up going on the cruise with me and Roy (which, by the way, we really enjoyed). However, he did ask lots of questions about the price, departure dates and locations, accommodations on the ship, etc., before announcing, laughingly, that he wasn't going to be able to go. Thank God! But it added to the weird dynamic between us. I mean, was he actually thinking of going at some point? Was he going to bring someone with him who either ended up not being able to go or never wanted to go or whatever?  Please don't tell me he was thinking of going by himself. Or had he really never intended on going and was just trying to scare me or find out exactly where I was going, when I was going, with whom I was going, etc.?  It was just more office weirdness.  I mean, to tell you the truth, there were times when Herman did seem overly interested in what some people in our office did during their non-work time.  On the other hand, it certainly seemed to me that with regard to Herman and me, that from almost the moment we met we really didn't get along.  In fact, I would go so far as to say it was ultra-clear to me that we didn't get along.  So why did he care about my personal or extra-work life at all?  Or was this just how all his personal relationships were, that he thought arguing with people and hassling people and not getting along was a normal relationship?  It's one more thing that I just never figured out.  But I did learn to refrain from suggesting to people at work that they go on a vacation with me unless I really wanted them to go on a vacation with me.

So, as I say, Herman, after scaring me, ultimately said he was "far too busy" to go on any cruises (Thank the Lord!).  Roy and I went on the cruise and had a really nice time, and by the end of July it was back to the normal routine at the Healthcare Facilitation Division at HSOO.

And then, once again, a few weeks later something very unexpected happened.

I was sitting in Herman's office.  The two of us had to talk to someone on the phone, so I had gone to his office with all my files and we called from there.  When we finished with this kind of lengthy phone call, I don't know, I think we were on the phone for 20 or 30 minutes, I was gathering up all my papers and was getting up to leave.  I stood up and Herman said something like, "Hey Matilda, you know there are at least two new restaurants that have opened up around here lately.  Why don't we try one of them sometime soon? I know you like to try different kinds of food, so how about this weekend?" I was, I think you call it, gobsmacked.  I mean, this is not a friend of mine.  I haven't agreed with virtually anything this guy has said since I met him, what's it been, a year and a half ago?

You know, you may be thinking that the normal reaction would be for me to think about Roy, his reaction, tell Herman no, this couldn't possibly work, my boyfriend wouldn't like it or would have to come with us, I'm busy, or something, but for some reason, my thinking, and my only or primary thinking was that I didn't want to have to sit through a dinner with Herman. No matter what other obvious suggestion or suggestions he might be making, the thought of dinner with Herman was just, let's say, not to my liking. I have had meals with Herman, usually not alone, but quite frequently several of us have ended up eating together, especially when we travel. I can't say every meal that included both Herman and me was terrible, but I don't remember much intriguing conversation either. Anyhow, my thinking was, for whatever reason, "Please, not dinner with Herman." I actually thought (all of this happens very fast when it happens) about suggesting lunch, but why do I have to go to lunch with Herman?

As I guess as had become a pattern, my quick thinking with regard to Herman, didn't work. I said, "Do you mean a bunch of us could go out this weekend?"

This seemed to annoy him. He said, "No Matilda, that's not what I said. I was suggesting that the two of us have dinner over the weekend. At one of these new restaurants."

You know, I know what my reaction was (I don't want to have to sit through a dinner with him), but I didn't know and honestly have never been able to figure out why Herman would think I'd be at all interested. So I said, "I don't know Herman, I'm not sure I want to try any of these new restaurants." I said this as I was looking down, rustling papers as much as possible, trying to seem preoccupied with very important work-related concerns, as well as trying to get out of there.

I thought I had done a pretty good job and not insulted anyone this time, but he continued. "Matilda," he said, "I know you told me you liked to go out to eat. We could do something else, what is it you like to do?"

I was floored. I said, "I don't know Herman, I really have a lot going on these next few weeks."

By then I was actually walking toward the door, and he said, "I would think you could make a little time for a little entertainment," or something like that."

Let me tell you one thing if this is not already obvious. I am not someone who is frequently at a loss for words, but this was a time that I was. My gut reaction, apparently not the best reaction, was to say "Look Herman, let's just forget the whole thing," but even to me, at that moment, it didn't seem like that would help the situation. I didn't want to offend him, I mean, come on, he's my boss, and we're really not getting along, but at least equally as much, I didn't want to go. And I'm old enough or experienced enough to have agreed to social engagements in my past that weren't fun, and I just don't think I should have to do this. And again, not to beat a dead horse, why on earth would this guy think I want to spend time with him? I have never given him that indication. Never. Ever.

I guess I just walked out of his office. I do think I said something on the way out, but I, for the life of me, can't remember what I said if I said anything. But I think I said something. My best guess is that, while walking away from him, i.e., my back was already to him, I said something like, "Well, it can't be this weekend Herman, but maybe we'll see how things go." But I don't want to bet my life or any limbs or anything that that's actually what I said. But I think I said something.

You know, I could be crazy, but it seems to me that when I left his office, Benita, whose desk is not *that* close to his office door, gave me a real funny look. But I'm not sure.

So, I went back to my cubicle, and thankfully it was just about time to go home. I couldn't see calling Roy from work where the walls may very well have ears, so I just pretty much left.

# CHAPTER 4

# *Rhonda*

When I got home, Roy wasn't around yet, so I called my girlfriend, Rhonda. I had known Rhonda since college, but we had lost touch with each other for years, and then run into each other again. Actually, someone we both knew had mentioned her in a Christmas card which caused me to call her and it has been just like old times ever since.

"Matilda, are you telling me that this asshole asked you out?" Rhonda asked, incredulous.

You see what I mean, I could always count on Rhonda.

"Yes," I said into the phone. "That is what I'm telling you. But I'm calmed down a little, and I'm hoping that this whole thing will just get forgotten."

"Tell me this again, Mattie. What exactly happened?" Rhonda went on.

"Well," I began, "I was in his office. The two of us had been on a kind of long phone call, the whole thing was over and I was getting up to leave. I stood up and he said something like 'Matilda, why don't we try some of these new restaurants around here? You told me you like to go out to eat, so how about this weekend?' I was completely surprised. I mean, come on Rhonda, why would this guy think I want to spend 10 minutes with him? I don't! We agree on approximately nothing. I don't want to have to sit through a dinner with him. I mean am I that attractive? (Just forget I said that.) So

I said, 'I don't know Herman, I'm not sure I want to try any of these new restaurants.' I thought that was that, but he said 'Matilda, I know you told me you liked to go out to eat.' Now when would I have told Herman I like to go out to eat? I don't remember ever saying anything that even comes close to that. And then, as I was leaving, he said something like, 'We could do something else, what is it you like to do?'"

"Oh my God," Rhonda interjected.

"I was just floored, Rhon. I said, 'I don't know, Herman, I really have a lot going on these next few weeks.' By then, I was actually walking toward the door, and he said, 'I would think you could make a little time for a little entertainment,' or something like that."

"Um, Matilda," Rhonda said, seeming to stretch out her syllables "this isn't good." "And," she went on," I don't think this is over."

"What do you mean?" I asked.

"I think this could blow up," she answered. "Have you told Roy about this?" she asked.

"No, I haven't had a chance to tell Roy. This just happened within the last hour or so. I don't know Rhonda, I think I'm just.. like.. completely discombobulated, or something" I said. "I felt terrible in that room, I can tell you that. I guess I feel like I insulted him. But why should I have to feel like I have to go to dinner with him? I really don't want to go to dinner, or anywhere else with him. How could he not know that? I guess I'll just try to block this out of my consciousness for now. I've got plenty of other stuff to worry about—I mean actual work-related stuff. Maybe we can just both forget this whole thing."

"Well, let me give you my opinion Matilda, for whatever it's worth," Rhonda said. "For your sake, I would like to believe that this'll just be forgotten, but I'm telling you, Matilda, these guys don't forget this kind of stuff. No matter how casual he acts and how casual you act, he's never going to forget this. And something could happen. Maybe it won't, but it could. That's the way I see it. And he is an ass, to put it mildly."

"Like what?" I asked. "Like what could happen?" I asked. Now I was incredulous and curious.

"Like you don't get a promotion or something," she replied.

"I don't know, Rhonda, I mean, I'd think that any kind of promotion for me is pretty far in the future. Doesn't that seem like kind of a big deal for just a dinner, or maybe no dinner in this case?" I asked, although honestly, I was feeling really kind of weird and unsettled. There was a little pause in our phone conversation. I may've been starting to feel a little sick or dizzy or something. I think I went to sit in a different chair.

Matty," Rhonda said "There's something I want to ask you. It's personal, but I'd like you to tell me the truth."

"Of course I'll tell you the truth, Rhonda, when have I not told you the truth?" I said.

"Matty, is there anything you're not telling me?" she asked.

"Like what?" I said.

"Like something between you and Herman? I mean, it's ok Matty. I'm fine with it. I mean, the guy sounds like a jerk, and you always make it sound like you don't like him, but is there something?" Rhonda asked.

"NO," I almost screamed. "Rhonda!" I said. "I am not pretending! The guy is a jerk. He's the epitome of an incompetent boss. He has been since I met him. When I met him, I couldn't believe he stood there talking about all the changes he was going to make to the office when he took over as if Angela didn't know what she was doing. No one likes him. He's an ass. Have I said that? Tanya hated him in Boise, not that that matters. I am not pretending not to like him. The guy runs around the office yelling out Bible verses and talking about how *he* bases *his* life on scripture! I mean where'd this guy come from? How did he get this job? I can't believe you'd even have that thought! The guy is a jerk." I think that's what I said. I'm really not sure.

"Well," Rhonda said, "you keep making it sound like he's a jerk and you don't like him and I believe you Matilda, but there have just been so many incidents. I'll say this though, I'd be careful who I tell about this, because someone could get the idea, or start some rumor that you somehow like this or want something to happen. People are weird, Matilda, especially about stuff like this. I mean, even after all the stuff I've heard about this guy, even I had that thought.  I don't think you're bragging, but I'm not working with you or competing with you at work.  It could seem like that to someone.  Especially someone who's not doing well.  It could happen.  And now that I think of it, are you going to tell anyone about this?  Like report it?" she asked.

"I don't know, Rhonda, I haven't even thought about that," I said.  "I think I need to hang up for now, Rhonda.  For some reason I think just talking about this now is getting me all upset."

"Sure, Matilda" Rhonda said.  "I'll talk to you later this week" and we both hung up.

I told Roy about the incident that night.  "Here we go," he said.

"What does that mean?"  I asked.

"The guy wants to have dinner with you, Matilda.  Maybe you should have dinner with him," he said.

"I'm not having dinner with him," I replied.  "Do you think this is a big deal, Roy?"  I asked him.

"It is what it is, Matilda," Roy replied.  Whatever that means.

"Well, I"m going to try to forget about it" I said.  "Do you think I should tell somebody?"  I asked him.

"Like who?"  he asked.

"Like report it," I said.

"Who can you report it to, Matty?"  he asked

"I don't know, H. R., I guess?  His boss?  Someone," I said.

"Well, you can," he said.  "I don't know if it'll do any good, but you can."  That was our very undefined conclusion.  "This isn't going to stop, Mattie," Roy commented.

I went back to work, and actually, things weren't that bad.  Herman was friendly, but not overly friendly.  He was gone at least parts of the next few days, and nothing was really awkward.  Things were actually relatively fine, but I was trying to decide whether I should somehow document this whole thing because God knows what'll happen in the future.  I did write a memo to myself on my computer and documented what happened and at least included dates, but I mean, it's not going to do much good if it just sits in my computer.

You know, if you go to any 12 – step program, they will tell you, and lots of people swear this is true, that once you start following the 12 steps, like being honest, making amends with people you've harmed, etc., good things start happening, just out of the blue. I'm not sure what the 12 - step people attribute it to (I think God, or maybe the universe), but, as I say, lots of people swear by it. Like suddenly, everything doesn't go wrong. Strangers start being nice to you, etc. My experience at work seemed to be like that, sort of, but in a different direction. I didn't think I was acting any different, or that Herman was, but weird things started happening. These were things that seemed significant, but I couldn't figure out how people could know anything about what had happened. So were these just coincidences with no connection to my new status (in my mind)?

Here's an example of what I mean. This incident with Karen occurred several days after the "Why don't we try some of these new restaurants" incident. I'm going to say it was less than a week later. Karen stopped by my cubicle and said, I swear this was out of the blue, "Matilda, have you ever had a boss that bothered you?"

Now, how would you answer that question? I swear she walked into my cubicle and asked me that.

I wondered if she was trying to tell me that Herman was bothering her. But how could she possibly know about my conversation with Herman? Did Benita hear something? On the other hand, Karen had never minced words about Herman; it seemed to me that if she had a complaint, she'd tell me the complaint. But why would she walk into my cubicle and say that? Three or four days after this whole incident with Herman?

So, back to my question, how should I respond to Karen? 1: Yes, I have one now. 2: Bother me in what way? 3: They all bother me. 4: Is someone bothering you, Karen?

So I said, "Well, you know Herman bugs me, Karen, so that's at least one." I was kind of chuckling as I said that.

This is what she said, I'll never know why. "I just keep hearing all these stories Matilda, about these people who like, hate to go to work because their bosses are so bad, and I really can't imagine it." And with that, she left my cubicle.

# CHAPTER 5

# *Mr. Kitterley*

I had been thinking about reporting this incident with Herman to someone for about 2 or 3 weeks, and I guess doing quite a bit of moaning to Roy about it when I decided I really needed to report this to

H. R..

I went upstairs one morning and asked to talk to the manager of H. R., Mr. Kitterley. "What is this about?" Margaret, his secretary, asked.

"I just need to talk to him about something.  I just can't say," I told her.

She didn't look very happy. "Well, I'm not sure he's going to see you about nothing," she said.  I didn't think that was the most professional response I'd ever gotten, but that is how things go sometimes.  So, I waited.

After a while I said, "This is a work-related situation, Margaret," trying to clarify.

"He's busy with a bunch of appointments, and he has two conference calls today, do you want to talk to Clarissa Sanborn?" she asked.

"Who is Clarissa Sanborn?" I asked.

"She's in charge of medical benefits," she said, "but she's really nice."  I couldn't believe it.  I mean, if Mr. Kitterley is too busy to see me and won't make some kind of appointment, I think he'd pass me off to someone with a little more relevant experience than someone who works with medical insurance. I mean, what is this?

"It's a somewhat sensitive situation, Margaret" I tried to explain, "and I'd really think I should talk directly to Mr. Kitterley."

"I don't know, Matilda," she said. "I can only see what he says." Thinking about it, during my time working for HSOO, I had seen Mr. Kitterley a lot. I had seen him at meetings, he has given little talks about changes in policies, etc. and I see him walking around, in the lunchroom, in the parking lot, etc. I never got the impression that he was *that* busy. So how does it turn out that when I want to have a short conversation with him, he's somehow way too busy?

After what seemed like a long time, I think it was probably 10 minutes, Margaret said, "He says it's okay, Matilda, so go on in." I was relieved that I hadn't agreed to tell this to someone in charge of medical benefits.

Mr. Kitterley was suddenly all business. I don't know what on earth he thought I was going to tell him. I mean does he have people stop in with complaints all the time? If he does, it's certainly news to me. I've never heard anyone say anything about going to talk to him about almost anything. I sat down in one of the chairs in front of his desk. He looked up. He pointedly didn't say anything. I had a weird feeling, and it wasn't good. Several moments passed, and then I started talking. "Good morning Mr. Kitterley" I said.

"Good morning, Miss Gundalini," he said perfunctorily.

I got up, closed his door, and walked back to the chair. "Mr. Kitterley, I work for Mr. Braddock downstairs in healthcare facilitation," I said, questioning my decision to come and talk to him.

"Yes," he said, whatever that was supposed to mean.

"The other day, I was in Herman's office, and he asked me out," I said. It was surprisingly hard to say that to him, but I think it was his not-very-nice attitude that was causing me to be so uncomfortable.

"Are you sure?" he said. For some reason, I felt like I should strap myself to some rocket and send myself to the moon. What do you mean, "Am I sure?" This wasn't going the way I had expected.

"Yes, I'm sure," I said in an irritated tone, because I was irritated and my irritation was increasing.

"So how is your relationship with him otherwise?" he asked. I kind of thought this was a business question, but I wasn't sure.

"It's relatively terrible," I said. "Or maybe I should say, "It's bad," I told him.

"So what makes you think he asked you out then?" he asked.

I was kind of floored. "Because he asked me out" I answered him. I had planned on having to explain what had happened, and I was going to try to not say too much, but I hadn't expected to have to explain what it meant to be asked out. This wasn't going well. "I was sitting in his office, and he asked me to go try some of these new restaurants around here," I said.

"So he didn't actually ask you out," Mr. Kitterley said.

"What do you mean he didn't ask me out?" I asked him.

"Well, Ms, Gundalini, people do go to restaurants," he said. This was really tanking.

"Mr. Kitterley, my boss asked me out and I don't think that is at all appropriate," I said.

"Well, what did you tell him, Ms. Gundalini?" he asked.

"I told him I didn't really want to go," I said.

"And has he continued to ask you out?" Mr. Kitterley asked.

"No," I responded.

"So, this is not actually harassment then," he said, and I felt he was hurrying me out of the office.

I felt very much like I was losing in this conversation, so I just thought I'd try from a different angle.

"Mr. Kitterley, is it normal for a supervisor to ask one of his subordinates to go to dinner?" I asked.

"Well, I'm not sure it's unusual for people to go out to eat, no I don't," he replied.

"But it kind of put me in an awkward situation, Mr. Kitterley, I mean this is my boss. I really *didn't* want to have dinner with him," I said.

"Ms. Gundalini, Did Mr. Braddock force you in some way to have dinner with him?" he asked. "It doesn't sound like it to me."

I'm not sure I said anything.

"So Ms. Gundalini," Mr. Kitterley said, "Do you want to file a complaint?"

"What kind of complaint?" I asked.

"A harassment complaint," he said. "I assume that's why you're here."

"Well, what would happen with a harassment complaint?" I asked. I had never heard of a formal harassment complaint, but I guess I had some idea that this would require me to submit some written something at some point.

"It would get investigated," he said shortly.

"You mean someone would investigate to see whether or not he asked me out?" I asked.

"Yes, Matilda, that's right," he said as condescendingly as possible.

"But that's not the problem," I said. I was astonished at how this conversation was going.

"Well, what *is* the problem then, Ms. Gundalini?" he asked.

"The problem is that it's inappropriate," I said. "I mean, we were alone. He was suggesting we get together for dinner over the weekend. I asked him if he meant to include other people and he said, 'no.'

I shouldn't be pressured like that."

"I hardly think you were being pressured, Ms. Gundalini," Mr. Kitterley said, "but if you'd like to file a complaint, Margaret can get you the form."

So now I'm in a situation I didn't expect. I think this is the type of thing Roy was predicting. I can file a complaint, Herman will have to be told find out about it and that might make things worse, or I can *not* file a complaint, and whatever happens in the future, there'll be no record anywhere, (except my note to myself in my computer) of anything leading up to whatever it is that might happen in the future.

"What do you recommend?" I finally asked him.

"It's not up to me, Ms. Gundalini. If you'd like to file a complaint about your supervisor you are free to do so. At any time.

And we will investigate.  And if we find a problem we will take the appropriate action," he said.

I really wasn't understanding what he was talking about.  It seemed like he didn't want me to file the complaint, but I wasn't sure why.  I mean it couldn't be that they had so many complaints about Herman that they didn't want another one, could it?  If there were many complaints about any supervisors at HSOO for anything, it was news to me.  I did know that Tanya hadn't liked working for Herman, but she never mentioned a formal complaint.  And Karen had never said anything about someone having complained.  So why would this H.R. professional be trying so hard not to have to tell Herman to behave?  What was going on here?

"I guess I'll take a form with me then," I said.  "But I do have a question."  Mr. Kitterley said nothing.

"Who exactly would do the investigation?"  I asked.

"This office would investigate," he said.

"So, is there a group of people who do this?"  I asked.  I still can't believe I asked him that.

"What are you asking, Ms. Gundalini?"  he asked me.

"I'm just wondering Mr. Kitterley, is it one person, is it a group of people you pick from, or is it like, the same group that investigates all the complaints?"  I asked.

"This office will conduct the investigation," Mr. Kitterley said to me.  "If you'd like a form, Margaret can give you the form," he said.

I really didn't know what to do.  It didn't sound like there was going to be much of an investigation, but I hated to not document anything.  I decided to just think about it for a few more days.  I didn't ask Margaret for a form on my way back to my desk.

That evening, Rhonda called.  "Well," she said.

"Well, what" I replied.

"Well, did you report that big jerk of a boss of yours?" she asked.

I took a kind of deep breath.  I'm not sure why.  "I started to Rhonda, but if you want just the facts, the short answer is 'no'" I said.

"What on earth does that mean?" she asked.

"I went to H.R. this morning, and the guy couldn't have been less inviting," I told her. "He repeated, like I was taping him or something, that I certainly had a right to file a complaint, but he acted like it was not believable that any boss would ever do anything weird," I said. "He didn't seem like he wanted to discuss it, and in fact, he wouldn't even give me the form or talk about it – he just kept telling me I could get one from his secretary."

"I guess I'm a little surprised, Matty, but I still think you should report it," Rhonda said. We talked about this whole thing a little more, and then the coversation turned to a number of other things, including the herb garden Rhonda's sister's was growing in her kitchen, and then that was that.

I hadn't gotten a form from Margaret on my way out of Mr. Kitterley's office, so I hadn't turned in any kind of complaint, but Herman seemed to really be annoyed with me after I had this conversation in H.R. Everything I said or did seemed to annoy him. The extra little jobs continued, the denigrating jabs in front of other people, and just overall being nasty, never having anything positive to say, just kept going on. I starting thinking about work a lot during my off hours, wondering what was going to happen the next day, etc.

# CHAPTER 6

# *Going to the Country*

It was now toward the end of September we had to get ready for our annual evaluations. Each of us had to prepare a page-long or so description of what we'd accomplished since last fall, with the more actual statistics (measurable accomplishments) we could include, the better. Once we turned that in and Herman wrote each of our evaluations, including these summaries of accomplishments, we'd each meet with him individually for 10 – 20 minutes, discuss our work, and make goals for the upcoming year. I had finished my summary and went to turn it in to Herman, but his office was dark. Benita saw me and said that Herman was going to be out of the office for several days, that he had gone to headquarters in Pennsylvania for some kind of planning session, and it looked like he might be there the rest of the week. I left the summary of my year's accomplishments in his inbox, and I guess felt a sense of relief that I could be free of Herman for a few days.

Later that morning, Roy called me at work. "Matty, I have an idea" he said. "Why don't we drive to my brother's cabin this weekend? If we both take off Monday and Tuesday, we could drive up Saturday, be there Sunday and Monday, drive back Tuesday, and be back at work Wednesday. It's getting to be about as late in the season as we can go, but the weather is supposed to be nice and I think it'd be fun. What do you think?" he asked.

"I think that sounds like a great idea, Roy. Let me take off next Monday and Tuesday. We're not that busy at work and I think getting away might be just the thing," I said.

"Honestly, Mattie, I kind of think you *need* to get away from that office for at least a couple of days. This next week is a good time for me to get away, and then I don't know when we'll have another chance to get away for a while," Roy explained.

So, I filled out my form to ask for the 2 days off early next week and saw that Herman had sent an email to all of us. When I read the email, it was so Herman-ish, I'm sure I was shaking my head in what had become my usual response to any business-related decisions by Herman. Herman had written to all of us saying he'd be out of the office for the rest of the week. He said he had to be at headquarters and what they thought they could accomplish in a day or so was now obviously going to take at least 2 or 3 days. Prior to meeting Herman, I had thought that usually in an office, when the boss was away he or she would leave someone in charge, at least for administrative tasks. But Mr. Braddock never wanted anyone else to be in charge so he wrote in the email to call him on his Blackberry if we needed to talk to him. I don't know why Herman did this, but he always did this. It ensured, in my opinion, that you'd call him while he was in the middle of something important so either you'd be talking to him about something important in front of a bunch of other people or he'd get mad that you bothered him. But, as you can see, he continued to insist that we call him directly. Anyway, I picked up the phone and called his number. I really didn't know how he could've gotten all the way to headquarters already. He was in the office yesterday and didn't say a word about being out of the office today. He usually told us when he wasn't going to be in, so it seemed like this was something last minute. I don't know how he was able to make travel arrangements so fast and get there (if he was already there), but he and Benita seemed to think he was either at headquarters or on his way.

He answered the phone with "This is Herman Braddock."

"Hey Herman, this is Matilda. How are you?" I started out.

"What can I help you with?" Herman asked, in a not really unusual manner.

"I'd like to be off Monday and Tuesday next week," I explained, "and I didn't know who else could approve my request since you're not here," I explained.

"Your request is denied," he said matter-of-factly.

I thought he was kidding. I mean, I hadn't realized it, and I know this is a request for time off not a demand, but all of us get lots of vacation time, and taking a day or two is actually less disruptive than taking a week or two off. I hadn't even considered the possibility that I couldn't have two days off in the not-busy season.

"No really, Herman," I said, "do you want me to just leave this request in your inbox since it doesn't seem like I'll see you before Monday?"

"I said your request is denied, Matilda. There's no reason to leave any request anywhere," Herman said in a not - joking voice.

"You're kidding," I blurted out.

"Why would I kid, Matilda. No, I am not kidding. I need everyone there next week," he said.

"Why?" I demanded.

"Because Matilda, next week, we have to complete these end - of - the - fiscal - year reviews, and I need everyone to be there," Herman explained.

I was flabbergasted. End of year reviews take not longer than 20 minutes and are not done as a group. He can't possibly be ready by Monday,. I don't even think most people had even given him their summaries, and I'd still be available all day Wednesday, all day Thursday, and all day Friday. We only need 20 minutes. He's got to be kidding.

I tried to explain all this. "I said 'no', Matilda," Herman said. I'd never heard of anyone being denied a few days off, except possibly when we were swamped and we are not. I was getting a very sinking feeling.

"Well, what would you do if I got sick?" I asked.

"You better not get sick," Herman said. "I need you all there all next week. Is there anything else you need?" he asked.

I just couldn't believe it. The weekend away with Roy was ruined. There was absolutely nothing earth-shattering (or less) that I had to do at work early next week. It would be a perfect time to take off a couple of days, a perfect time for the cabin, and Roy could get away, which wasn't always the case. And it's going to be ruined over a 20-minute end - of - year review? Unbelievable!

"Good-bye, Matilda," Herman said. "I'll see you Monday."

"But Herman wait," I said, but he hung up. I just couldn't believe this.

A little while later I was coming back to my cubicle from the copier when I ran into Karen. "What's the matter with you?" Karen asked. Apparently, I didn't look great.

"Herman denied my request for two days of vacation time next week. He said we all had to be here for the end - of - year reviews," I explained.

"What!" she exclaimed.

I repeated, "He said I couldn't be off Monday and Tuesday because everyone had to be here next week for end - of - year reviews."

"End - of - year reviews don't take a week!" Karen said.

"I know that, Karen," I replied.

"You should've asked Elise," Karen said.

"Elise!" I yelled. "What does Elise have to do with anything?" I asked.

"Elise can approve vacation time when Herman's not here," Karen said.

"Since when?" I asked. I felt like crying.

"She can do it," Karen insisted.

"I have never heard of that," I said, as my sinking feeling continued.

As luck would have it, Elise came walking around the corner. I think we were actually both staring at her. Elise was one of the most senior healthcare facilitators, but I have never heard even a whisper of her being able to do any of Herman's job while he was away. "Do you need some help?" Elise asked both me and Karen. I re-explained the situation. Her mouth didn't drop open, but her eyes did get pretty wide. "He needs everyone one here all week?" she asked, seemingly very surprised.

"Yes, Elise, I am not allowed to be off Monday and Tuesday because everyone has to be here all week to do end - of - year reviews, " I re-explained.

"You must've misunderstood him, Matilda," Elise suggested, "These reviews aren't due for close to a month."

"I wish, Elise, but he was pretty much yelling at me that I had to be here, no one could be off, and whatever else. He told me at least twice." I said.

"You know, Matilda, why don't you call him back? He must not have understood," she offered.

"He's just going to get mad," I said. "I don't see how he could've misunderstood. I asked him about Monday and Tuesday, and he told me in no uncertain terms that I couldn't be off and had to be here," it seemed like I was re-re-re- explaining.

Both Karen and Elise were now staring at me. "I just don't know what to tell you, Matilda," said Elise. "I've never heard of anything like this."

"So Elise, do you approved vacation requests when Herman isn't here?" I asked.

"Well, I can," she replied.

"I never heard that," I said.

"When Herman isn't here, someone has to sign, so I usually do it," she explained.

"That's news to me," I said and walked back to my cubicle.

I now had to tell Roy. I called him. He was as incredulous as I was. He said "Well, I guess the cabin is out. We're not going to drive all the way there for one day. We'll just have to concentrate on having a nice weekend here, Matty. The weather *is* supposed to be beautiful. We can think of something to do. But your boss is a real a-hole, Matilda."

"That I know," I said. "Thanks, Roy. I feel terrible."

"Don't worry about it, Matty. I've had bigger disappointments than this in my life. But it would've been nice," Roy said.

# CHAPTER 7

# *You Ain't Goin' Noplace*

So, after Herman refused to let me have two days off a couple of weeks ago (I mean, if I had died they would've gotten along without me), I started thinking more and more that I better file that complaint and at least document something.

I went back up to Margaret's desk and asked her for the form. I swear the color drained from her face. "You want to file a complaint against your supervisor?" she asked. She seemed incredulous.

"Well, yes, Margaret. I was here talking to Mr. Kitterley a few weeks ago, and he told me several times that it was certainly my right," I tried to explain.

"Oh, it's certainly your right, Ms. Gundalini, I'm not saying it's not your right," she said, cryptically, if you ask me.

Margaret rifled around in at least one drawer and through several manila folders and eventually found a form and handed it to me. She said something like, "If you turn this in, it'll be investigated" in what seemed to me like a very legalistic way. Anyhow, I took the form and went directly to the copier and made about 4 more copies, just in case. The title on the form was "Report of Offensive, Inappropriate, or Concerning Behavior." I glanced at it, and it didn't seem like a very hard form. In essence it asked some questions like my name, some contact information, who exactly I was saying had exhibited this behavior, and then there was a big blank space for the "employee" to explain the situation. It said clearly at the bottom "Anyone witnessing or feeling they have been subjected to Offensive, Inappropriate, or Concerning behavior on the part of any person employed by or connected with Health Solutions and Office Oversight, Inc. should feel free to report such actions to the Human Resources (H. R.) department, preferably in writing, and preferably by submitting this form. The Human Resources department will promptly investigate any such reports. Employees reporting such behavior should expect a response from the Human Resources department within 6 weeks from the date of the report."

I worked on the wording for my "complaint" at my desk, then printed out my draft and took it home.

I worked on it a little more that evening. The only incidents I described were 1) that my supervisor, I gave the date when we were alone in his office, had asked me to go to dinner with him over the weekend, referring to "these new restaurants" near our office, and then I decided to add in  2) a brief description of my request for two days off being denied after that "asking out" incident when I had never heard of any similar request being denied. That wasn't exactly true. Some people were denied time off during our busy season, but I thought I'd keep it simple. I read what I had to Roy. He thought about it for I'd say about a 20 seconds. Then he said, "You should report it, Matilda, because they need to know. Once it's in writing, maybe they'll have to do something about this guy. But they might not, I mean, they haven't so far."

"So honestly Roy, what is the outcome you think I'll get?" I asked.

"I don't know, Matilda. I really don't know. They've got to know about this guy. The guy you talked to sounds like he doesn't want you to report it, and he's the one who should be talking to your boss. So I just don't know, but it sounds like your pal Herman knows where the bodies are buried."

"But you think I should report it?" I asked, although he had just said that.

"Nothing's going to happen if you don't," Roy said, "but you just might not get the result you'd like."

So that was that. I finalized the report, made some copies, and turned it in toward the end of that week.

Oh, My God!

A few days later, Herman walked over to my cubicle and didn't look happy. He said, "Matilda, I understand you've been up in H. R. talking to Dick Kitterley about me."

Well, I had to say something. I think I said "Well, not exactly about you" (lie!). "It was more just about my job" (another lie!).

I think he sort of snorted and left. I do know it was a short conversation, if you want to call that a conversataion. And It wasn't relaxing.

I don't know if it's possible to like your job if you really don't like your boss. I thought I liked my job, but I was starting to realize that I was almost dreading going to work. So, I started paying a little more attention to email notices we got from H.R about job openings. In some cases, with certain approvals, it is possible to move from one job to another at HSOO non-competitively.

I saw a couple of openings over the next few weeks that normally I would never have considered, but, given my current circumstance, I actually responded to two or three, at least indicating that I was interested.

After responding that I was interested in the third one, I got an email from Catherine Deerfield from the finance department, thanking me for my interest and asking about setting up an interview.

The next morning Herman appeared at my cubicle. "So, Matilda," he began, "I understand you've applied for a job in another department," he said.

I didn't really see any reason to be ashamed about this. I can't get fired for trying to transfer to a different position, can I? "Which one?" I answered, I guess a little condescendingly.

Herman's eyes widened noticeably. "The financial specialist position," he said authoritatively.

"Yes, I did," I said, trying very hard to keep my voice even.

"Well, I disapproved your transfer," Herman said. I'm sure my mouth dropped open. How can he *disapprove* a transfer?

Noting my surprise, I guess, Herman continued, "You can still go to the interview if you'd like Matilda, but I told Mr. Kitterley that you were not available for a transfer."

"Why would my boss be able to keep me from transferring to another position?" I blurted out, but after all, I did want to know.

"Because sometimes a department just isn't in a position to lose another person, Matilda," he answered. "I already have one vacancy," he said unconvincingly. I should've asked him if we just couldn't postpone the transfer. Our department did have a vacancy because one of the other healthcare facilitators had left HSOO completely for a different job, but that was months ago and Herman hadn't made the smallest effort to fill the position – I actually thought there had been a decision not to fill it.

So here's another conundrum regarding Herman – he seemed to be indicating, over and over, that I'm a problem for him and he wished I'd disappear (or something), and then when he has this golden opportunity to get rid of me, he's going to go out of his way to make sure I *can't* leave, which honestly, I don't think he can do. I started to feel like some kind of insect that some little kids are playing with. It couldn't be that the answer is to exhibit poor performance, so he'll let me go, could it? I began, at this point, to feel that my employment situation was definitely deteriorating, although I knew I was good at my job!

That night, my sister, Pella, called. "I think you should come home two weeks from Saturday," she said. "Louanny Loudenton is having a big 47th birthday party, and everyone is asking if you'll be there."

"Well," I said, "I might be able to do that. I haven't seen Louanny in ages." Louanny, Pella, and I had grown up together in Blackhawk, Kansas. Pella is three years younger than I am. Blackhawk is about 300 miles southeast of Rockleburg, so it's about a 5-hour drive. Given how actually close that is to where I live, it's kind of surprising that I don't see my family more than I do. But this might be a good excuse to go home. "I knew her birthday was coming up," I said, "but I really didn't know anything about a party."

"I've been running into her all over the place lately," Pella went on. "I saw her at the grocery store with her daughter who is 11 years old now. Can you believe it? Then I saw her at a baby shower for one of the girls I work with, and I saw her and her husband, Remy, at the park last week. When we met at the park, she mentioned that her birthday was coming up and she was thinking of having a big party. I think it's going to be at her cousin's big house out in St. George" Pella went on. "Of course she asked about you. Actually, she asked about everyone, including Daddy and Mom and the hardware store."

My grandparents immigrated to the United States from northern Italy in the 1920s, and ended up living in southern California. My grandfather was some kind of supervisor at an orange grove in Orange County when there were still orange groves there. This is unbelievable to me given his less-than-perfect English, but somehow, my grandfather, Giovanni, started working part-time writing or editing screenplays for the movie industry. Apparently, when my father was in high school and college, so in the 1940s, he also did some work like that for the movie studios. In the 1950s, my grandfather actually knew several of the people in Hollywood that were targeted by Senator Joseph McCarthy as communists and knew people whose careers and lives were ruined or looked like they were going to be ruined by these allegations. So, my grandfather decided he wanted to move away from California and really wanted to get "as far away from the movies" as he could. I think Rockleburg, Kansas did fit the bill. Anyhow, by the time the whole family moved, my parents were married and had a child, my sister, and a second one, my oldest brother, was about to be born. So my parents ended up managing, not owning, but managing, a hardware store in Rockleburg. They were managing it when I was born and were managing it when I left for college. All of us used to hang around there, sometimes stocking shelves or cashiering, but as I remember, my main "job" was helping people find specific merchandise in the store. I liked that, and I think I was good at it. Anyhow, everyone in town or at least everyone we went to school with, knew us as the family at Second Street Hardware.

"You know, Pella, maybe I will give her a call. It'd be nice to see everyone again. I can see you, and if everyone else isn't too busy, maybe they can squeeze me in for coffee or breakfast or something, too. Maybe I'll even take a couple of days off and make a long weekend out of it," I said. "Oh, I guess I should tell you though Pella, the last time I asked for a couple of days off, my boss denied it, so we'll have to see how this goes," I added. "But we're not that busy at work, so it should work. I'm sure Louanny won't mind me showing up."

"Your boss wouldn't let you have a couple of days off, Matilda? What happened? You never told me about this?" Pella asked.

"Well, you know I'm not on the best terms with my boss," I began.

"Actually no, I didn't know that," Pella said.

"So I asked for two days off, and he just denied it," I explained.

"I didn't know anyone at your office had trouble getting time off," Pella said. "Oh wait, I do remember you saying something about a busy season, and no one could get time off."

"No, it wasn't that, Pella," I said. "We were done with the busy season, I asked for time off, and he said I couldn't be off" I partly explained. "He really didn't have much of a reason. Oh and speaking of that, I applied for a different job, still at HSOO, and he blocked me from getting it. It would've been a transfer."

"What do you mean he blocked you from getting a different job?" Pella asked.

"Well," I started, "I'm really not getting along with this guy. He's kind of picking on me. So, most recently, we had this deal where I couldn't have two days off, and then I half-heartedly asked about moving to another department, and he came over to my cubicle and said he had the right to block it because our department was short-handed and he did" I said.

"What is this guy's problem?" Pella asked. "I've never heard of a guy keeping someone from another job. And if he doesn't particularly like having you work for him, I'd think he'd be having a party if you were leaving," she said.

"I can't really explain it, Pell. We aren't getting along, and a lot of weird stuff has been happening. I mean, I never liked the guy, and he's never been great to work for, but I think my whole job situation is deteriorating," I said.

"So are you looking for another job, Matilda? You haven't said anything about that," she asked.

"Well, not really, Pella. I mean, I actually like my job, and I don't think there are many other jobs at HSOO that I'd like as much. Most people don't travel as much, and we talk to a lot of different people and get involved in a lot of different situations, and I kind of like that. And I don't really want to have to leave HSOO. I guess I'm kind of hoping he'll leave," I said, although I hadn't really thought of that until I said it. "The whole reason I asked for the two days off was because Roy had suggested getting away for a weekend, and we just ended up not being able to go."

"That is absolute bullshit," Pella said.

"Pella," I said, "could we please watch our language?"

"I'm not kidding Matilda, that is really unfair. Why didn't you tell us? What else is going on at that office? I think you should complain about him. Is it hard for anyone else to get a couple of days off?" she asked.

"You know, Pella, I really don't want to talk about this anymore. The guy is a jerk. Everything at work isn't terrible, but he's a jerk. And I don't notice him getting any less jerkier," I responded. "So, can we just forget it for now?" I asked.

"We can forget it for the moment," she said, "but I need to hear more about this when you get here. You are coming, aren't you? I can tell Louanny if you want," she offered.

"I'm leaning toward coming, Pella. If I can get some time off work, I'll come for more than the weekend. Please don't blab this stuff about work to everyone, so this is the big topic of conversation if and when I get there. It's enough 5 days a week," I said.

"I'll only blab to a few people. But what does Roy have to say about all this? Do you still see Roy?" she asked.

"He's very understanding, and yes, we still see each other," I said.

"OK, Matilda, you can be excused.  I'm really sorry to hear that things are kind of crummy at work," she said.  "I know you used to really like that job."

"Good-bye, Pella," I said.

"Bye Matty," she said, and we both hung up.

# CHAPTER 8

# *Different Management Styles*

A few weeks later it was getting to be November, and Veterans Day is a HSOO holiday as well as a federal holiday. About a week before Veterans Day, we had a big, everyone-should-attend meeting in our cafeteria. Our director got up and thanked all the veterans, then Mr. Kitterley of H.R. got up and said HSOO thought it was important to honor veterans in this way (with a day off) and suggested we each do something nice for a veteran or for anyone for that matter. As we were leaving the room, I ran into Herman by the door, and I swear he made some comment to a few of us about how he hoped we wouldn't "drink too much" on our "holiday," whatever that was supposed to mean.

Late in the afternoon of Tuesday, November 10th, I got a call from Mr. Braddock asking me to come to his office. I walked into his office, and he was relatively nice. Actually, nicer than usual. I should've known something was off, but I just sat down.

Herman said, "So, how are you, Matilda? How are things going for you?" I didn't know what to say or to think. I mean, what was he referring to?

"It's going ok," I dragged out my answer. I really had no idea what he was asking about.

"Is everything ok with your job? With your home life?" he asked.

I didn't know how to answer. "Well, it's ok, Herman," I said. I started to say, "It's not perfect," but I stopped myself.  I didn't know where *that* conversation would go.

"Well, Matilda," Herman continued.  "The reason I've called you in here is that there's something I want to talk to you about."

"OK," I said, again dragging out the two syllables.  I was getting the feeling that this wasn't going to be good, but on the other hand, he did seem like he was trying to get to the point.  I waited for a shoe to drop, as it were.

"But I'm not ready," he said.  Now, haven't I been telling you that I frequently have a hard time understanding Mr. Braddock?  I don't know if I said anything or not, but I was just as confused as I was the day he told me to hurry up and make plane reservations to match his, and then he hadn't decided what day to fly.  I don't even remember if I looked at him or looked around the room or what.  I just know I couldn't figure out what this guy was doing.  Why call me into his office to tell me he wanted to talk to me just to tell me he's not ready to speak to me about whatever it is he wants to talk about?  Are we talking about me going to see Mr. Kitterley?  Or something completely different?  Herman recapped "So Matilda, do you understand?" he asked.  "There's something I want to talk to you about, I'm going to talk to you about it, but I'm just not ready."

I'm sure I made a face.  "So, Herman," I said, "you called me in here to tell me you want to talk to me about something, but you're not ready to talk to me about it?"  Herman looked pleased to me.

"Yes, Matilda, that's exactly it," he said.

I couldn't resist: "Well, Herman, why didn't you just wait until you were ready before you called me to your office?"  I asked condescendingly, but honestly, I wanted to know the answer to that question.

Herman looked crushed if you ask me.  "Because I'm not ready, Matilda," he said in a scolding tone.  "That is all," he added.

So, completely confused, I left and walked back to my cubicle.

On the way back to my cubicle, not actually that far from Herman's office, I ran into Mr. Mumford.  The healthcare facilitation department, of which Herman is the supervisor, is really a division of a larger department.  For some reason, we always call the facilitation department a department, although technically it's a division, but anyway, the head of the entire department, officially the Outreach department, is Mr. Mumford. Mr. Mumford is kind of a character, in my opinion. For a guy who's in charge of this multi-state region, he seems kind of shy. He doesn't really say much. I really only see him at official functions like meetings and luncheons, but occasionally, when I get a chance to talk to him, if I bring up some topic that's not work-related (and *not* sports!), we typically have a nice or nice-*ish* conversation. We have discussed 1) whether or not smallpox vaccinations are still necessary, 2) traffic on the way to work in Rockleburg, 3) (not political stuff), and 4) I can't remember, but I have, as I say, had nice conversations with him, mostly at the coffee pot or water fountain, as long as they're about anything other than work. So, we ran into each other, I mean, figuratively, in the office, and I don't know what I looked like, but he said: "What's the matter, Matilda?"

I hated to waste a chance to talk directly to the boss, but I was trying to work on being more tactful, so I had to think, and I think I said something like "Well, you know Mr. Mumford, I sometimes find Herman to be really hard to understand."

His smile disappeared. I think he breathed in and out. Then he looked right into my eyes and said: "Is this something we need to talk about, Matilda?" I had a distinct feeling that he was really hoping I'd say "no," but I didn't entirely want to pass up this chance.

I said, "I don't know if that's necessary, Mr. Mumford, but I really don't understand a lot of what he says." I thought he looked relieved. We were standing in an aisle in the middle of the office. God only knows who could hear us.

"I know he has a very different management style than what you might like," Mr. Mumford said.

I blurted out, kind of loudly "MANAGEMENT STYLE!" I mean, "oops." For the last what, two years, I've been telling myself that a big part of the problem is that Herman doesn't actually manage --he just does stuff, says stuff, etc. I've thought, frequently, that this is what parents talk about when they start talking about not having a manual about parenting, doing the best they can, not knowing what to do, etc. But this is a for-profit business, and many, many, many people go to school to study management, many people seem to just have a knack for it, and I don't think too many management schools suggest asking your subordinates to help you find a date, or getting in a LOUD argument in a restaurant about working at a fruit stand 15 or 20 years ago (or maybe more). Or getting into a LOUD argument with subordinates or former subordinates in a public (or private for that matter) restaurant *about anything!* I did not know this was considered a management style. Anyhow, Mr. Mumford kind of excused himself and walked past me toward his office. Maybe he hurried toward his office, I'm not sure.

So I got back to my cubicle, and a few hours later, Karen stopped by and said, of all things, "So, have you heard about Herman's poker parties?" Well, no, I haven't. What could this all be about?

"What poker parties?" I asked. Again, this office is not that big, and our cubicles are fairly open, and lots of people hear lots of things. I usually find out about what someone has overheard much later, typically at an inopportune time.

"Well, Herman and a bunch of guys have poker parties on Friday nights," she responded.

"What guys?" I asked.

"I'm not exactly sure, Matilda, but I know it's not us," she said. I was just looking at Karen, and I feel that I had a quizzical look on my face. She took another spoonful of something she was eating out of a paper cup.

"Herman and some guys from Finance get together for poker. I don't know if it's every Friday, but some Fridays. And we are definitely not invited" Karen explained.

"Finance?" I said. "I have never seen him anywhere near people from finance."

"I don't think it's only finance," Karen said. "I heard this from Margaret," she went on.

"Margaret?" I said. "You mean Margaret, Mr. Kitterley's secretary?" I asked.

"Yes," Karen said. "I was talking to her, and she was complaining about being left out of stuff and said something about Mr. Kitterley and a bunch of people had started getting together for poker a few months ago.  Then she mentioned that she had heard that recently Herman had joined their group.  Just keeping you informed," she said as she left my cubicle.

Now, I don't exactly know what to think about this.  If Herman wants to play poker (which I kind of doubt), I mean, is that my business?  Or my concern?  On the other hand, any private conversations Herman has or may have with Human Resources does make me a little nervous.  And, well, I get it, these games are at somebody's house, so they aren't exactly open.  I have never seen Mr. Kitterley with anyone from finance, and I certainly have never seen him with Herman, so it's kind of an odd group.  Also, I have heard Herman, frequently, walk around the office talking about how religious he is and how he wouldn't dream of gambling.  Like he couldn't possibly buy a lottery ticket.  So is he getting involved primarily for the gossip or informational aspect of these poker (or any other) get togethers?  It's nutty, but it could be.

So, Veterans Day came and went.  Roy is a veteran, not that I can say we actually celebrated, but we did make a nice dinner at home, and it was a nice enough day.

I really don't remember if it was the same week as Veterans Day or the next week, but somewhere in there, Herman called me into his office.  "You know Matilda, I know you have kind of a community spirit, don't you?  He asked.  I immediately thought he was going to put me on some kind of a committee, something to do with the Rockleburg community—maybe a holiday parade or help feeding the homeless, hopefully not cleaning up some river or something.

"Yes, Herman," I replied.  "I do think I have a kind of community spirit.  At least I'd like to think so" I thought I was being self-effacing.  I mean, I've been involved in *tons* of community projects in my life, election stuff, blood drives, membership drives for non-profits, all kinds of stuff.  Since high school!  Of course, I like to help my community.

"Well, there's a project that needs to be done" Herman continued, "and it would really help out the department, and I thought of you right away."

I was actually feeling flattered. "Ok," I said, anticipating some great opportunity where I could shine.

"We need you to clean out the file cabinets," he said. I'm sure my happy demeanor changed.

"Clean the file cabinets?" I said, incredulous. "Me, like by myself?" I said. I think I was starting to feel faint. We had *tons* of file cabinets, and I think I knew what he meant. He meant, go through each drawer, consolidate files where necessary, don't necessarily look at each page in each file but dispose of obvious duplicates or old, unnecessary stuff, and then re-label everything. This job had been done before. It wasn't an annual thing, but it was a BIG, dirty job and basically a full-time job for *at least* two or three weeks. As I recall, now that I'm thinking about it, I think they hired temps for this or had volunteers from some other offices come here to do it. It certainly wasn't healthcare facilitators, and it wasn't our clerical staff that had done this in the past. And as I recall, these people, I don't know, maybe it was 3 or 4 people, they were here for *weeks!* Is this guy kidding? I mean, I do agree with him on one point, and that is that having cleaned - out file cabinets, and disposing of stuff we don't need really does make it easier to just use the files, but this is *my* job now? I mean, once again, Are you kidding?

I think I'd call it flabbergasted. I didn't know what to say. For some reason, I thought of having to tell this to Roy, and I imagined him saying, "You didn't agree to this, did you?" I just couldn't. So I said, "Herman, do you mean me, by myself, go through all these cabinets and throw stuff away?" I was trying to make the point that this is a lot of work, and surely he didn't realize it when he gave or tried to give me this assignment.

"Yes, Matilda, that's what I mean," he said. "It would really help out the department, and let's face it, you're good at it." He was smiling. I think he actually said something like, "Well, we could have someone else do the re-labeling once you've finished with the re-organizing." It didn't make me happy to see his smile.

"Is anyone else going to help?" I said, knowing immediately that it was a mistake, because that made it sound like I was agreeing to it.

"Well, perhaps," he said (I knew he was acting, but I couldn't do anything about it) "if it comes down to that, we might be able to find you some help."  Now he was really smiling "But I really want this to be *your* project, Matilda.  This may really be your calling."  Now I knew this was some kind of negotiation.  He's trying to get me categorized as someone who doesn't deserve a thinking job, but more of a doing job, that requires not too much planning.  He's thinking that that would show I'm incapable of anything that involves cognition.  I really did not want to agree to this.

I don't know why I said this, but I did.  I said, "Does Mr. Mumford know about this?"  Mr. Braddock's smile disappeared, as some might say, "in a big hurry."  I mean, he went from beaming to despondent very, very rapidly.  Now, *that* made me happy.

"Why would you ask that Matilda," he asked, and before I could answer, he said, "no, we have not discussed it."

I think I was starting to feel a little wobbly, or faint, or dizzy or something.  I'm pretty sure I took a very deep breath.  Then, I guess as many people could've predicted, but I didn't, the whole, let's say, atmosphere in the room changed.  Significantly.

"You know," Herman said, "I have about had it with your attitude, Matilda."  I was, if not stunned, very surprised.

"What do you mean, Herman," I said innocently, and I actually meant it.  I mean the guy was just telling me about my community spirit, how he had thought about me right away for a special project, etc., and now I was a problem.  I mean, just like that.  It's possible it should've been obvious to me, but it wasn't.  I did bring up his boss, I know that, but come on, clean out the file cabinets for a month or more?

Then Herman went on, "I think it's time for a warning," he said.

"A warning?"  I questioned.  "A warning about what?"  I asked, and I was not playing around.  I didn't know what he was talking about.  A warning about bringing up his boss?  Why can't I bring up his boss?

"Don't give me that," Herman said.  I felt that we were kind of entering a new kind of language between the two of us.  This was kind of more, I don't know, threatening or personal or something. This was just a different way that Herman was talking to me than had ever happened before. "You go back to your cubicle, Matilda, and we'll talk later," he said. "I'm going to write up something, and we're going to agree on a few ground rules, and this attitude of yours is going to stop."

I really was very surprised. Don't tell me this guy, this completely incompetent boss is going to call me into his office, tell me he personally selected me to do a really demeaning, below-my-job-level job, me and only me, that's going to take weeks and surely keep me from doing my actual work, so he can complain about that, and then have the nerve to tell me I have an attitude? I just wasn't going to let this go.

"What attitude?" I asked. I thought he looked like he might punch me. He looked, to put it mildly, not at all happy. This is not any indication of a "different management style." I mean the guy calls me in, I am not a beginner or an intern or someone just out of college, thinks he's going to trick me into agreeing to some really menial, dirty work that's going to take a long time, and now that I think about it, no one else in the whole building has ever been told to do, and when I don't agree he gets mad? This is not management. It might be abuse, but it's not management. It is not a management style.

"Your attitude!" he almost screamed. "Your insubordinate attitude, Matilda!" he said (loudly). Now I was sure people could hear. "It's going to stop!" he continued.

I don't know if I would've been better off to just leave or not, but I didn't. I said, and I wasn't yelling, because I didn't realize what was going on (and I still don't to be honest) "I am not insubordinate, Herman. I don't know what you're talking about." He kind of looked like he was going to have a stroke. So *then* I left. I was actually kind of proud of myself for not agreeing to the cabinet cleaning thing.

# CHAPTER 9

# Surprises and the Corcoran Account

It was about this time that I got a call from Mr. Kitterley, who said: "Ms. Gundalini, I am calling to let you know about our internal investigation regarding your complaint about your supervisor."

I actually felt kind of excited. "This'll be great!" I thought. Herman will be reprimanded, we'll have a normal workplace, and it'll all be because I courageously brought all this up. "Yes," I replied into the phone, anticipating the great news.

"The human resources department has completed its investigation, Ms. Gundalini, and you'll be getting a letter in the mail explaining the results," he began. "But I wanted to touch base with you and let you know that as far as we're concerned, we are closing this case and considering it complete."

I didn't exactly know what he was telling me. I mean, what did it mean for Herman? And what was going to happen going forward? And I really couldn't articulate it at the moment, but what if there was some kind of retaliation?

"So, the committee agreed with me?" I asked, stating the obvious.

"As I say, Ms. Gundalini, you'll be getting a letter explaining our findings. I just wanted to let you know," he re-stated. I wasn't getting this.

I hated to hang up the phone. I said, "Well, but Mr. Kitterley, was there actually a committee that looked into this?" I asked. I thought I heard some kind of exasperated breathing over the phone. I started wondering why he hadn't asked me to come up to his office, I mean, it's not like it would've been any trouble or anything.

"As I've told you, Ms. Gundalini, this office has investigated your complaint, and the investigation is complete. We have mailed a letter with the findings to you at your home. And HSOO now considers the matter to be closed." It didn't seem like there was any reason to go on.

"Ok, thank you," I said.

"You're welcome, Ms. Gundalini," Mr. Kitterley said and hung up.

It seemed like immediately Karen appeared in my cubicle. "What was *that* about?" she asked.

I knew I should avoid telling her any specifics, and especially since now we all know that at least some people are listening. I tried to be careful, but secret-keeping isn't my strong suit. "Oh, it was Mr. Kitterley from H.R." letting at least one cat out of one bag. Her eyes widened.

"Oh," she said, inviting me to provide more information.

"I had talked to him a few weeks ago, and he was just letting me know they were done..." I tried not to finish that sentence, although I was well aware that my answer wasn't making any sense. And I felt, real or not, that the office had gotten noticeably quieter and people must be listening.

"Did you file a complaint?" she asked forcefully.

"A complaint about what?" I asked, doing my best FBI agent impersonation, and just by the way, how does she know there's a complaint process?

"I don't know," Karen said, outdoing my law enforcement technique. "Matilda, what's going on?" she asked.

Now HSOO, even with Herman, has always been a really nice place to work. It's a little less so (or maybe more than a little) since Herman showed up, but I do know Karen well enough and my sometimes-loving-to-gossip co-workers well enough to try to keep this a little under cover, even though I already had the sense that my situation wasn't exactly covert. I decided to go back to whatever I was working on. As far as I could tell, Karen continued staring at me, then said, "Well, there's plenty to complain about Matilda, but you do have to be careful when your boss already has it in for you," and she exited my cubicle. My mouth had dropped open, but I didn't have a chance to say anything.

I'm going to have to get her away from the office and ask her about what she knows or thinks she knows," I thought. "That shouldn't be too hard."

The next day Herman came over to my cubicle with an enormous smile on his face. "Matilda," he began, "I'm going to need you to work on the Corcoran account."

"The Corcoran account?" I asked.

"Yes, Matilda, the Corcoran account," Herman said. "The Corcoran Account" refers to a clinic in Oklahoma. One of their administrative assistants got arrested for DUI a few months ago and had a small amount of marijuana on her, and now this month, a nurse who works there has been arrested for having a shed full of marijuana at her house. This was a juicy enough story that everyone in our

healthcare facilitation department (division) had heard about it. "As you know, Matilda, all of the principals at the clinic are swearing no knowledge of anything related to either of these incidents," Herman said. "They fired the administrative assistant and the nurse, and well, you're going to have to talk to them," he went on. "I believe the nurse is saying the marijuana was found at a house she owns but had rented out. She claims she had no idea of anything that was being kept in the shed in the backyard. The tenants have disappeared, and she didn't exactly have a lease. We're just going to have to investigate and document what is going on there," he explained.

Now, *this* is right up my alley. I love talking to people about these juicy stories. You always get so much scoop. It's interesting. And then for some reason, he added: "Of course Matilda, you're still responsible for all of your other work, and since there may be travel involved, it may curtail any time off you may've had planned."

I absolutely did not know what he was saying. He continued to have this gigantic, uncharacteristic smile on his face. This kind of assignment really wasn't anything weird. The travel, if I needed to do that, wasn't unusual. So, in a way, this was a normal assignment, just a little juicier than some. I would guess that this investigation is something that wouldn't normally be assigned to me, but maybe I'm wrong. Perhaps it is a little more responsibility than I've had in the past, but why would he start saying I can't have time off? And mentioning my other work? I mean, there are only so many hours in a day. These are administrative issues, I don't think anyone is going to die if my investigation takes 4 weeks instead of 2 ½. I didn't want to conclude what was the obvious conclusion that this had something to do with my complaint, but I wasn't understanding this. On the other hand, I hadn't understood a lot of what Herman had tried to tell me ever since I met him.

The next day, when I got home, there was a letter waiting for me from HSOO, Human Resources. I was, I think you could say, gleeful. I opened it up and started reading it. Well, so much for glee. It was a one-page letter, or maybe more like a  one-half page letter, that said:

"Dear Ms. Gundalini:

This office has received and investigated your complaint of inappropriate behavior on the part of your supervisor, Mr. Herman Braddock, toward you. We find that your complaint has no merit. If you'd like to have this decision reviewed, you should contact the vice president for the Mid-America Sector, Mr. Rowman. You should include a copy of your original complaint and a copy of this letter.

Sincerely,

Richard Kitterley

Manager, Human Resources

Mid-America Sector

I did not feel good.

I told Roy about it that evening. "Well, you have your answer, Matty," he said.

"What answer?" I asked.

"They're not going to do anything," he responded.

"Now what?" I thought aloud.

"Just go to work and do your job, and your boss is going to continue to hassle you," he said.

"Are you saying I should look for another job?" I asked him.

Roy said, "I'm saying that as long as what's-his-name, Herman, is your boss, he's going to continue to hassle you. They are not going to do anything. Do you want me to go there and talk to him?" Roy asked.

"No, I don't want you to go talk to him, Roy, that's ridiculous," I said. I mean, how silly is that? I am a professional woman, and I have to have my boyfriend go to my boss and tell him to leave me alone?

"Well, at least you know the story now," he said. "You've got it in writing. It's too bad, though. They really should stop this. But they're not going to. I wonder how many other complaints they've ignored? You're probably not the only one, Matty," he said.

I had a sad feeling. This kind of thing doesn't normally happen to me. I get along with people. I've worked with lots of people. Of course I've heard of people in bad situations where there's just not an easy way out, and I've read about these kinds of stories, but now I'm in one, and I just don't know what to do.

"Well, I guess I'll just go to the vice president and see what he has to say," I said.

"Good luck Matilda," Roy said unenthusiastically.

"Are you saying I shouldn't?" I asked.

"I'm saying it's not going to matter either way, Matilda. Nothing is going to happen. Everyone already knows about your boss and they are not interested" Roy explained.

I may need to talk to Rhonda.

Later that week at work another weird thing happened, but weird incidents between Herman and me had already become pretty much a very usual occurrence, so was this weird or was it usual? Well, it seemed weird to me then, and still seems weird to me when I think about it.

I was sitting in my cubicle when I got a phone call. It was Herman. He said, "I'm at the airport Matilda, but I locked the keys to the HSOO car in the car. My briefcase is in the trunk. I need you to get a duplicate key from the people in vehicle administration and come here, get my briefcase and the key out of the car, and bring them to me. My flight leaves in about an hour. I'll wait by the security line."

"What on earth is this guy talking about?" I thought.

"Herman," I began, "You want me to come to the airport right now, find your car, get the briefcase, then find you and bring it to you?" I asked. I was incredulous. I mean, just the idea of me trying to get to him in time was ridiculous, but he's got a secretary. How is this *my* job?

"Yes, Matilda, that's what I said. Why are you repeating everything?" he asked. It was sort of like a comedy routine.

"Herman, it's going to take me an hour to get the key and get to the airport!" I said loudly.

"I guess you'd better get a move on then, Ms. Gundalini!" he said.

"But Herman, how am I going to find you in the airport?" I mean, I just knew this wasn't going to work.

"I told you Matilda, I'll be waiting by the security line," he said, apparently thinking this was helpful.

I tried again to get out of this. "Herman, how am I going to find your car?" I said, but I felt like I was losing this battle.

"It's in the H section, Matilda. Where we always park!" he seemed to be getting mad.

"The H section!" It's possible I was yelling now. "The H section is kind of big, Herman," I said, but somehow, I knew I just better get going, that this was probably not going to work, and that somehow it would be all my fault.

"Oh, you'll be able to find it, Matilda. You can recognize the car. It's silver," he said and started laughing.

"Are you sure you want me to do this, Herman?" I asked. I mean, there just wasn't very much time.

"Someone has to work on the Corcoran account, Matilda, you certainly don't seem to be making any progress," he said.

"THE CORCORAN ACCOUNT!" I said, and now I was yelling. Are you going to Oklahoma about the Corcoran account? I asked.

"Yes, Matilda. Do I have your permission?" he said sarcastically.

"But Herman, I thought you wanted me to work on it?" I said, really kind of crestfallen.

"Well, no progress was being made, so I'm here with Pam, and we're going to Oklahoma to work on it," he told me, not gently.

I absolutely could not believe this. Pam was another healthcare facilitator, but she really didn't have that great of a reputation within the department. If he wanted to go with her and train her, that's fine, but the two of them already made travel arrangements and are at the airport, and no one said a word to me? I mean, to be honest, I had begun to think this was kind of an interesting situation, and I was really disappointed that I wasn't going to get involved. But Pam? And no one saying anything? I mean, he only told me about it last week. The travel arrangements alone had to involve Herman, Pam, probably Benita, and God knows who else—and locking the keys in the car? What on earth were the two of them doing?

"I'll go try to get a key and come to the airport Herman, but I don't really think there's time," I said.

"There better be time, Matilda," he shot back.

This really had the makings of a disaster, but I went upstairs, and after having to wait what seemed like many minutes while someone looked up which car Herman had and tried to find a duplicate key, I did get a key. There was well under an hour before he had said his plane would take off, and it would probably take me at least a half-hour just to get to the airport. This'll never work.

You know, this whole situation where Herman comes to work in Rockleburg, we don't get along and everything else I've been telling you, happened in the first few years of the 21st century. Cell phones were not quite as universal as they later became. I actually did have a flip phone, but it was a recent acquisition. I didn't know Herman's Blackberry number by heart and I was sure he didn't have my new number, because I had only given it to a few people On my way out, to this very-unlikely-to succeed assignment, I stopped at

Benita's desk to ask her for his phone number rather than run back to my cubicle.

She gave me the number and said, "If you don't mind me asking Matilda, where are you going?" she asked.

"Herman wants me to drive to the airport.  He said he locked his briefcase in the trunk and locked the keys in the car.  He wants me to find the car and get his briefcase and the keys to him, and I guess Pam," I reported.

"Again!" she yelled.

"What do you mean?" I asked. (Airport or no airport, I had to know).

"Last week he had some neighbor pick him up from somewhere, and he left his sweater in the neighbor's car.  When he realized he didn't have it a few days later, he actually asked me to drive to the neighbor's house and pick it up," she said.

"Did you go?"  (This information was far more important than getting to the airport.)

"Well, it was better than sitting here," she said.  I guess that was a "yes."  How am I being left out of all this office scoop?  That's what I'd like to know.

"Well, I gotta go, Benita," I said.

"Do you have enough time?"  She asked.

"I really don't think so," I said.

"Well, why even go?"  she asked.

"'Cuz he told me to," I said.  She shrugged her shoulders.

When I got to the exit for the airport, I was sure his plane was taking off.  I couldn't see the point of continuing this.  I didn't know what to do.  I decided to try to call Herman, hoping for some kind of reprieve.  I pulled into a parking lot and called the number Benita had given me.  Herman answered.  Anyone could've guessed how this conversation was going to go.

"Where are you?" Herman barked.

"I'm just getting off the expressway, Herman," I explained.  "I don't know what you want me to do."

"Undependable Matilda," he said, "that's what I'm going to start calling you."

"I'm undependable?" I said, again incredulous, but that was getting to be my feeling almost every time I talked to Herman.

"Yes, undependable Matilda," he said. "You know Matilda," he continued. "I could've called any one of my healthcare facilitators, but I chose you. I guess that was a mistake."

I decided not to be so helpful. "It was a mistake?" I acted like I didn't understand. This seemed to annoy ol' Herman.

"Yes, Matilda, that's what I said. A mistake. I chose someone who just can't follow instructions," he insulted me.

"Should I keep coming to the airport, or are you going to leave without it or ..." I didn't finish.

"Just meet me at the car, Matilda. We'll miss this flight and try again tomorrow. But don't think I'll forgive you," he said. "I needed you in a pinch, and you didn't come through."

"Forgive me?" I thought. "Forgive me for what? For wasting the company's gas coming here?"

"Ok," I said, "Bye, Herman." I started the car up and drove the remaining few miles to the airport. It's not really that easy of a drive. As far as other drivers, no one knows where they're going, everyone is nervous about making flights, etc., but I did find Herman and Pam in the parking lot by a silver HSOO car. I gave Herman the key (thank God I didn't leave it on Benita's desk). Pam was grinning from ear to ear. "Hi, Pam," I said, as nicely as I could.

"Oh, hi, Matilda," she said. Honestly, I couldn't really remember the last time I had heard her voice.

Herman opened the car door and retrieved his original key from the console. Then he opened the trunk and got his briefcase out. Later, when I was going over this scene in my mind, I couldn't figure out why he took the briefcase out of the trunk. I guess he wanted to put it somewhere where he might see it and remember it back at the office. In fact, why had he put it in the trunk at all?

Anyway, we were getting ready to leave and Herman said: "Well, let's get going, Matilda, some of us have work to do back at the office." I didn't exactly know what that was supposed to mean, but I was sure it wasn't good.

# CHAPTER 10

# *A Parting of the Ways*

We left, me in my car and Herman and Pam in the silver WSOO car. They seemed to be very happy as long as I wasn't anywhere near them – joyous almost.

We all went back to the office, and things went back to what had become usual. I was apparently no longer working on the Corcoran account if there actually was a Corcoran account. I don't think Herman ever went to Oklahoma or the airport or I don't know. If Pam was involved in anything with this clinic in Oklahoma, I don't know anything about it. My best information is that there were a few phone calls between Herman and the clinic in Oklahoma, and something or other got worked out. I don't know any more than that.

I told Roy about this whole thing, and he said, "There was no plane trip," which I kind of believe.

I told Rhonda about it, and she just kept saying, "Oh my God" and "Oh my God, Matilda." I mean, what more is there to say? I could've asked Benita for more information about whether there really was a plane reservation or what was going on, but I just didn't feel like it. The only other thing that happened related to this which kind of irritated me was that the next day, the woman from vehicle administration called me asking for the duplicate key for the silver car.

"I gave it to Herman Braddock," I said.  I don't know if I was raising my voice or not, but I was annoyed.

"Well, we don't have it," she said.  "Could you please get it to us this morning?  We really don't want to lose those keys."  Can I just say, I get that?  No one should need this extra key in the first place.  It really didn't have anything to do with me, but somehow, I'm going to be the problem.  I went to ask Herman for it, he started laughing, pulled it out of his pants pocket, and handed it to me.

"You've got to remember these things, Matilda," he said.  I don't know whether my mouth dropped open or not.  Things seemed very weird in Herman's office right now.  I mean, we all know that for the past 2 years, since Angela left and Herman showed up, things have been weird , but now I felt like we were entering a new level of a twilight zone.  Please don't tell me every day is going to be Denigrate Matilda Day, *and* I'm going to have to compete with Pam of all people.  To be honest, I mean, we're all nice about it, but Pamela is lucky if she can remember what she's supposed to be working on, much less how to get it done or how to get it done on time.  How could this be happening?  And, on a related note, I had been noticing that I was now frequently waking up about 3 or 3:30 in the morning and thinking about what was going to happen at work.

As a last effort, at least the only thing I could think of, I went to see Mr. Kitterley one more time.  I realize he hadn't been sympathetic in the past, to put it mildly, and he probably wasn't going to be now, but maybe he could somehow direct me.

Margaret allowed me to go into his office to see him.  "Hi Mr. Kitterley," I said as cheerfully as I possibly could.  He was actually a little bit nice.  Or nicer than last time.

"Hello, Ms. Gundalini," he said, "What brings you here this time?"  Not to be paranoid, I did wonder if this was somehow being recorded or someone was listening or watching somehow.

"Well, you know Mr. Kitterley," I started "I just want to tell you about something.  The other day Mr. Braddock called me from the airport and said he had locked the keys in his car..."  I wasn't finished, but Mr. Kitterley, who by the way was all smiles now, was waving his hand at me. I guess he wanted me to stop talking. I wasn't sure.

"Ms. Gundalini," he began, "let me share something with you that I think may put your mind at ease."

What on earth could this be? I thought. Please don't tell me Herman told them to never let me have a duplicate key or something like that.

Mr. Kitterley went on, "Mr. Braddock has accepted another position at headquarters and will be leaving this facility in the next few weeks," he said. He looked like he thought he had just told me I'd won some kind of lottery. I think I was starting to feel dizzy.

"He's leaving?" I kind of muttered. Then I said, I don't know why, "for another position?"

"Yes, Matilda, may I call you Matilda?" Mr. Kitterley asked. He went on, "His promotion has been finalized, so I feel that I can share this with you. I'm sure he'll be announcing it to your division very soon. In fact, I was just working on the paperwork to advertise the vacancy for the supervisor of the healthcare facilitation division."

I didn't scream, but I wanted to. "Promotion?" I said, and I know I had a very quizzical look on my face.

"Yes," Mr. Kitterley said, and I'm telling you he looked *very* happy.

I guess you'd call this blurting out, "Why would he get a promotion?" I asked.

"Mr. Kitterley looked much less happy. "Because he deserves one, Matilda. Now, doesn't that help you with some of your concerns? You know Matilda, all of us at HSOO want *all* of our employees to have a comfortable workplace."

I thought I had gotten used to my workplace existing in some kind of a twilight zone, but maybe now this was *the* twilight zone. I don't know what it means when you can't recognize whether you're in a twilight zone or not.

I think I was starting to feel a headache coming on. I don't really remember how we ended this talk, but I left and went back to my cubicle. I wanted to tell Karen this very hot scoop, but I don't know, I think the phone rang or something, somehow I got busy doing something, and I didn't exactly what to steal Herman's thunder anyway, if this was going to be his big announcement.

Very late that afternoon Herman sent out an email. The subject line was "Healthcare Facilitator Supervisor Position Opening." Herman went on in a fairly brief email to talk about how any of us could apply for the position and then led into it being at this facility and then mentioned that he'd be leaving. He was a little vague about when he'd be leaving, but he did say he was going to accept a promotion to a job at headquarters in the office of diversity.

I could hear people reacting around the office: "Yay!," "Oh my God," "What?!," "Well, I'll be." Then I quit listening.

Karen walked over and said, "Did you see Herman's email," apparently wanting to see my reaction.

"Yes," I said, not happily.

"What's wrong, Matilda," she said, "maybe we'll get another Angela."

I just sat there.

"What's wrong?" Karen repeated.

"It's a promotion, Karen," I explained.

"Yeah, I know," she said. "So what?"

"It's sickening to tell you the truth," I said.

"Why" she seemed to be genuinely confused.

"Because he's incompetent!" I repeated what may've become my mantra.

"Oh, so what," she said. "He'll be gone."

"We don't get promoted, Karen, and we work hard," I said, not really addressing the subject.

"Well, it's a done deal as far as I can see," Karen said. "I think we should have a party."

I just didn't feel very party-ish.

I told Roy about it that evening, and he said, "That's how things go, Matilda. I know it's not what you wanted, but at least he'll be gone. Maybe you'll get someone even worse," he said, chuckling.

# EPILOGUE

I felt confused quite a bit during the next few weeks, but in a different way than Herman had trained us to expect.

Apparently, Angela had called someone in our division, and said that the reason Herman had gotten the job here in Rockleburg in the first place was because of problems between him and his new boss in Idaho. Supposedly, his boss in Idaho was at some kind of regional office, not the same building Herman (and Tanya) were working in in Boise. She was very unhappy with Herman, according to the Angela story, and had started pressuring him or documenting stuff or giving him some kind of ultimatums about a number of things, not the least of which were problems with his subordinates. According to the rumors at the Rockleburg HSOO office, the boss (no name was given, at least to me) she was threatening to fire him, but headquarters didn't want to, so when Angela announced her retirement, they thought Rockleburg would give him a fresh start. So, they "moved" him to Rockleburg which, due to the size of the office, was a promotion. That, in my opinion, is annoyingly good luck.

What is the deal with Herman? I just couldn't figure it out. With all the business majors graduating from colleges, couldn't they find someone who knew what he or she was doing? Or wasn't someone ever going to tell Herman to behave like a grown-up? I guess not.

I ran into Mr. Murdock a couple of times at work during the weeks between when Herman had announced his promotion (he always referred to it as a promotion, not a move) and when he actually left.  Mr. Murdock acted very much like Mr. Kitterley, seeming to think I'd be thrilled to see Herman leave.  "But Mr. Murdock," I said, "it's a promotion."

I know he knew what I was saying.  He tried to look surprised and said: "What's the difference, Matilda?  He'll be out of your hair."

The final time I actually said to him, "You know, Mr. Murdock, he's going to behave the same way in Pennsylvania," and he actually replied, "Yes Matilda, but he'll be in Pennsylvania."